D0066054

AMERICAN REFUGEES

AMERICAN REFUGEES

TURNING TO CANADA FOR FREEDOM

RITA SHELTON DEVERELL

Printed and bound in Canada at Friesens. The text of this book is printed on 100% post-consumer recycled paper with earth-friendly vegetable-based inks.

Cover design: Duncan Campbell, University of Regina Press
Text design: John van der Woude, JVDW Designs
Copy editor: Donna Grant
Proofreader: Kristine Douaud
Cover art: Source image: "American grunge flag" by lambada/iStockphoto. Modified by Duncan Noel Campbell.

Library and Archives Canada Cataloguing in Publication

Title: American refugees : turning to Canada for freedom / Rita Shelton Deverell.
Names: Deverell, Rita Shelton, 1945- author.
Series: Regina collection.
Description: Series statement: The Regina collection
Identifiers: Canadiana (print) 20190053739 | Canadiana (ebook) 20190053763 | ISBN 9780889776258 (hardcover) | ISBN 9780889776265 (PDF) | ISBN 9780889776272 (HTML)
Subjects: LCSH: Americans—Canada—History. | LCSH: Canada—Emigration and immigration. | LCSH: United States—Emigration and immigration.
Classification: LCC FC106.A5 D48 2019 | DDC 325/.2730971—dc23

10 9 8 7 6 5 4 3 2 1

University of Regina Press, University of Regina
Regina, Saskatchewan, Canada, S4S 0A2
tel: (306) 585-4758 fax: (306) 585-4699
web: www.uofrpress.ca

U OF R PRESS

We acknowledge the support of the Canada Council for the Arts for our publishing program. We acknowledge the financial support of the Government of Canada. / Nous reconnaissons l'appui financier du gouvernement du Canada. This publication was made possible with support from Creative Saskatchewan's Book Publishing Production Grant Program.

Canada Council for the Arts   Conseil des Arts du Canada   Canadä   creative SASKATCHEWAN

*To the people of Saskatchewan who created a
home for this immigrant from 1971 to 1989*

*Sue and Ken Kramer, founding artistic directors of
the Globe Theatre, who cast me on the main stage
and the school tour without talk of race.*

*Canadian Broadcasting Corporation's Dave White, who made
my brown face "the face" of the Regina Noon TV show.*

*The University of Regina's School of Journalism and
Communications, which appointed me the first woman to
lead a journalism program in a Canadian university.*

*The city of Weyburn, Saskatchewan, which asked this
immigrant to give keynote remarks at the transformation
of Calvary Baptist Church, the former church of Tommy
Douglas, to the Tommy Douglas Centre for Performing Arts.*

CONTENTS

EPILOGUE
Build on It   235
My Story Continues: American No Longer

ILLUSTRATIONS

ACKNOWLEDGEMENTS

Excerpts from some of my previous writings, productions, and broadcasts have appeared in other publications: "Epilogue," in *Fists Upon a Star: Memoir of Love, Theatre, and Escape from McCarthyism*, by Florence Bean James and Jean Freeman (Regina: University of Regina Press, 2013), 237–58; *McCarthy and the Old Woman* (play for two actors), copy script (Toronto: Playwrights Guild of Canada, 2008); "Slavery Endangers the Master's Health, but Please Don't Shoot the Messenger," in *Cultivating Canada: Reconciliation through the Lens of Cultural Diversity*, Aboriginal Healing Foundation Research Series 3, ed. Ashok Mathur, Jonathan Dewar, and Mike DeGagne (Ottawa: Aboriginal Healing Foundation, 2011), 383–96; *Smoked Glass Ceiling* (one-woman show), copy script (Toronto: Playwrights Guild of Canada, 2006); and "Who Will Inherit the Airwaves?" (speech), *Canadian Journal of Communications* 34 (2009): 143–54.

I am grateful to the following authors for giving me permission to quote from their works in this book: Matthew Behrens, Steven Bush, Frank Canino, Dan David, Sylvia D. Hamilton, Bonnie Sherr Klein, the estate of Mavor Moore, John Merritt, and Carol Whiteman. Their full citations appear in the Selected References.

For absolutely everything, I am deeply thankful to the University of Regina Press: the editing intelligence, insight, and sensitivity of Sean Prpick, Dallas Harrison, and Donna Grant; the constant support and enthusiasm of publisher Bruce Walsh for the ideas of this book; and all on the URP team for putting their publication shovels in the ground at exactly the right moment in Canadian/ American history.

Finally, I am in a family of artists who write, paint, illustrate, perform, and teach, all on deadline. Their indulgence of me has gone way beyond not stomping out when I behaved irrationally while working on this book. Thank you son Shelton Ramsay and partner Rex.

INTRODUCTION

ALLEGIANCE TO ALL HER HEIRS AND SUCCESSORS

A CANADIAN CITIZENSHIP CEREMONY, 2017

This is not a fantasy. This is the truth. On July 14, 2017, I stood in front of a packed courtroom in Scarborough, Ontario, wearing a black robe, about to swear in ninety-eight new Canadian citizens. Behind me was the Royal Coat of Arms, known formally as the Arms of Her Majesty the Queen in Right of Canada.

Those of us who are not citizenship judges (a paid job) but have the authority to be voluntary presiding officers, in my case because I am a Member of the Order of Canada, are actually called "Eminent Canadians." I have a couple of friends who have also presided at the ceremony, and they warned me it is an emotional experience. One said she completely lost it and sobbed while administering the Oath of Canadian Citizenship. I quipped, "I'm an actor and only cry when paid to do so."

Wrong. I got through administering the oath in English in a firm, confident voice. In French, I wasn't so assured but didn't have time to cry while worrying about pronunciation. I thought I was home free!

Wrong. It was shaking each individual's hand, presenting the new Canadian citizens with their citizenship certificates, and saying "Welcome to Canada" that got to me. Since these words were simply said to one person at a time, maybe they didn't notice I was tearing up. Plus, what to say to each new citizen is the presiding officer's decision, and I didn't think my choice would bring on my tears until it happened.

How on earth and in heaven did I get to be the person saying "Welcome to Canada"? How did I, suddenly, it seemed almost by magic, become the presiding officer who had the power, the right, the permission, the responsibility, to say those three words?

I certainly never dreamed of "eminence" in 1967 when I immigrated to Canada. In fact, I just hoped to cross the border safely via the Peace Bridge between Buffalo, New York, and Fort Erie, Ontario. In the station wagon stuffed with wedding gifts, rented by my just-married, born-in-Canada groom, I was certainly chasing a brand-new, hopefully successful, life in Canada. But eminence? Never in my wildest dreams could I have projected that fifty years later a little black girl from the American South would say "In the name of Her Majesty the Queen, I welcome you" at the beginning of a citizenship ceremony.

RCMP Constable Russel and Rita Shelton Deverell, Citizenship Ceremony, 2017 (Courtesy Joanne Wesolowski)

In much less heartwarming recent news, in the evening of November 8, 2016, as it became clear Donald Trump would be president of the United States, the website of Citizenship and Immigration Canada crashed. Although there had been many jokes during the long campaign about Americans moving to Canada if Trump won, this was no joke. The site was presumably overloaded with those seeking information on how to walk in the footsteps of earlier "American refugees chasing the Canadian dream," some of whom we'll meet in this book.

In the heat of this post-election moment, it might have appeared that something new and dramatic was happening. Actually, though, the website crash was the same old, same old: a 250-year-old story with a cyberspace gloss. American citizens and others resident or captive in the country that promotes itself as the freest, most prosperous, and most egalitarian in the universe were forced to question whether they could remain there. That question has been raised many times before—from the Revolutionary War to the War of 1812, by travellers on the Underground Railroad, by victims of "un-American activities" trials, during the black Civil Rights movement, by Vietnam War resisters, then by Iraq War resisters. And now. Could the Citizenship and Immigration Canada website searchers of 2016 stay in a country that had a demonstrably long, tragic, and blatantly unresolved history of racism? Equally long-standing warmongering? Right-wing tests of American loyalty? Little quality universal public education, health care, and arts support? And could they stay in a country that takes all criticism as disloyalty, punishable in various ways, including incarceration?

Canada has a visibly different history when it comes to these issues. To be more accurate, Canada has several different histories, depending on the era, the party in power, the need for immigrants with particular backgrounds, and, most importantly, how sovereign Canada feels itself to be at the moment.

Personally, I thought I'd successfully and finally escaped the United States in 1967 when I got my Canadian landed immigrant's card, for sure by the time I took the Oath of Canadian Citizenship in 1975.

Wrong. On New Year's Day 2015, at six o'clock in the morning in the Miami airport, my greatest desire being a place to brush my teeth, my recapture by the United States happened. I was on a brief layover there while returning from a trip to Santiago, Chile, where my husband, Rex, and I had visited our son, before returning "home" to Canada's largest city. At least five border guards took a serious interest in my valid Canadian passport. Having lived in Canada for nearly fifty years, I felt secure in my Canadian citizenship, but since it was early New Year's Day there were very few travellers in the airport, and US border control officers apparently had lots of time to interrogate me. My Canadian passport was electronically scanned and it accurately indicated a birthplace in the United States, Houston to be specific. This seems to have been the signal to detain me and inform me that I was still a "US person" and had to enter the United States with an American passport. I was assured that "The United States still loves you." Rex, meanwhile, was quickly flagged through because his birthplace was Toronto.

Rex Deverell and Rita Shelton Deverell, 2018 (Photo by Shelton Ramsay Deverell)

Plans for this book had been made two years before day one of 2015. Yet this catalytic incident increased my writing speed. It became clear to me that Canada-US relations were in another turbulent period. Philosophical and political differences were heating up, as they have, on and off, throughout our history on this shared continent. And these differences became clear to many ordinary citizens through increasing challenges at the border.

The harmonious Canada-US border is legendary. On both sides of it, we go through long periods of pontificating about how much alike the two countries are, what a great friendship we have, how we're the biggest trading partners, and how dependent we are on each other for defence and therefore for peace.

This love fest, seriously impaired by 9/11, and further called into question by the aftermath of the Trump win in 2016, glosses over the periodic waves of American immigration to Canada, all of which have been triggered by major differences of philosophy and policy. These sometimes substantial differences over how the world should be run, and how we should conduct ourselves as citizens, are lived by both individuals and groups who immigrate (or flee) to Canada.

In the immediate aftermath of the 2016 US election, our trade relationship was underscored: Prime Minister Justin Trudeau immediately said, "Canada has no closer friend, partner, and ally than the United States," and he looked forward to working with Trump's administration and the US Congress on trade, investment, and international peace and security.[1]

By the summer of 2018, however, Canada-US relations took a sharp downturn, with accusations of "backstabbing" behaviour aimed at Prime Minister Trudeau by President Trump. Trudeau, in turn, promised that Canada would not be pushed around by America. By and large, labour unions, other politicians, and Canadian citizens appear to support the prime minister. And it is hoped that this period will be seen in the post-Trump future as a weird and wacky interlude in an otherwise peaceful coexistence between two continental neighbours.

Individual stories of immigration and residence comprise the subject matter of this book. *American Refugees* introduces us to "refugees"—both literal and figurative—from the United States living in Canada. The United Nations defines a refugee as "someone who has been forced to flee his or her country because of persecution, war or violence. A refugee has a well-founded fear of persecution for reasons of race, religion, nationality, political opinion or membership in a particular social group. Most likely, they cannot return home or are afraid to do so."[2]

From the American Revolution to Vietnam to Iraq to today, many American immigrants to Canada have met that definition, though seldom have they been formally classified as refugees. This book explores the multiple reasons why these refugees and/or their descendants stayed in Canada after the particular crisis had passed (for example, after the un-American trials were over or after there was an amnesty for Vietnam War draft resisters). And I chronicle these new Canadians' major contributions to Canadian society and how, in most cases, they have vigorously supported the cherished differences seen in politics and culture between Canada and the United States. American expatriates become especially active when they see threatened the distinctions that caused them to become born-again Canadians.

To be crystal clear, all of the American expats profiled in this book are, or were, people with deep convictions, integrity, and great love for Canada, their new country. I underline the love because these expats have also been critical of Canada, usually for reasons that Canadians born in the country do not quickly see: erosion of our much-praised universal health-care and public education systems; dwindling support for the arts and Canadian-owned cultural industries; deportations of contemporary war resisters; racism directed systematically at Indigenous peoples and sporadically at people of colour; and the bedrock colonialism of the country. Despite this list of serious problems, the people profiled in this book all decided to stay in Canada. Some could have returned to the United States, but they chose to remain in their adopted country. Their criticisms stem from love and dedication.

Also, importantly, there are Indigenous peoples to consider. They aren't immigrants or expats, and most aren't refugees in the classical sense, but they have major, long-standing difficulties living on both sides of the world's longest undefended border. Centuries of mistreatment, manipulation, and misunderstanding by both American and Canadian governments have made many Indigenous North Americans feel, in effect, like internal refugees on this continent. For some, the alienation that has come with their bitter experiences has strengthened their sense of belonging to sovereign Indigenous nations, standing apart from the dominant political power structures. My conversation with journalist Dan David, a proud Mohawk, will shine light on these Indigenous cross-border truths and explain why loyalty to Canada, which surrounds the territory of his First Nation, is not uppermost in his mind.

As of this writing, we do not know how history will judge the immigrants and refugees from the United States in the years immediately following the 2016 US election. We do know what happened prior to 2016, and we can consider the stories of a few of the individuals who have come to call Canada home. We can ask how a relatively small group of American expats living in Canada have stood on guard for generations to defend that long undefended border. This book asks what they defended in each era, how, and why. Who knew that the United States "still loves" those of us who turned our backs on Uncle Sam? The descendants of Loyalist refugees from the Revolutionary War and the War of 1812, travellers on the Underground Railroad, those blacklisted by the 1940s and 1950s Un-American Activities Committees, Vietnam War resisters, marchers to Canada during the black Civil Rights movement, and those forming "a coalition of the unwilling" against the wars in Afghanistan and Iraq in the 2000s: these people were not and still are not loved by the United States. The hostility has in fact been obvious.

Back to the airport in Miami. Why, then, this sudden declared affection in 2015? Short answer: because just maybe, among the more than 375,000 American expatriates in Canada, some lucrative "tax evaders" will be found. That's the relatively recent and odd policy saga of Canadian citizens who suddenly find out that the United States still deems them "US persons." "Are you kidding?" was not what I said to the US border guards on New Year's Day 2015. Humour didn't seem to be an appropriate or useful response. "The US still loves me?!" But that certainly was the retort in my head.

Reviewing the facts of my biography, I don't seem to be all that lovable to the United States: born in 1945 in the Houston Negro Hospital; married in 1967 in New York City to a white guy, while Texas still had anti-miscegenation laws; immigrated to Canada in its centennial year and thereafter have been an artist/broadcaster/social activist; became a Canadian citizen in 1975, joyfully swearing loyalty to Her Majesty Queen Elizabeth II (we were both younger then, Her Majesty only fifty); and under the impression that I had relinquished all other citizenships. I have earned money, owned property, and voted only in Canada, and I have had only a Canadian passport. Further, I was made a Member of the Order of Canada in 2005, an honour available almost exclusively to Canadian citizens, in part because of my work at Aboriginal Peoples Television Network (APTN). With this racial background and activist professional history, the real question is, "When did the United States *start* to love me?" I think I missed that nanosecond and, along with many others, became what's now called "an accidental American."

The attention directed at expat Americans and their earnings on foreign soil had been prompted at least partly by the US administration's passing of the Foreign Account Tax Compliance Act (FATCA) in 2010. Subsequently, there was pressure from the US on financial institutions around the world to provide information about bank accounts and earnings of US citizens living elsewhere, including in Canada. In early 2016, *iPolitics* reported that during the federal election in 2015 Revenue Canada had "quietly handed" 155,000 Canadian banking records over to the US Internal Revenue Service, "without waiting for an assessment from Canada's Privacy Commissioner or the outcome of a court challenge to the controversial move." About 150,000 of those records related to US residents or to people with US citizenship living in Canada.[3]

Given that Trudeau and the Liberals won the 2015 election, and especially after the 2016 Trump Republican win, this particular tax skirmish is unlikely to get much more, if any, attention. The United States and Canada have much bigger differences and more serious relationship hurdles. But I will briefly mention the obvious. Since all Canadian citizens, whether born in Canada or naturalized here, are supposed to have the same rights and responsibilities, handing over financial information on some Canadian citizens to the United States creates two-tiered citizenship. Viewed with the hindsight of 250 years, this tax skirmish is but a small illustration of Canada's true relationship with the United States. The various "wars" throughout our history (Revolutionary, 1812, Fugitive Slave Act, Cold/McCarthyism, Civil Rights, Vietnam, Afghanistan, Iraq) have tested whether Canada can afford to assert its sovereignty and how far it can be asserted in any given battle. On a sliding scale, our differences and sovereignty go from 0 to 100. As a country, we like to remember the 100 percent Canada-is-independent events and forget the less brave episodes.

The moment the United States declared its love for me and others like me—or at least its love for our tax dollars—might have been brief indeed: that is, if the 2016 presidential voter analysis is accurate, the election was decided primarily by white men. Was it perhaps other types of American citizens who crashed Citizenship and Immigration Canada's website?

Successful paths taken by refugees and immigrants from the United States to Canada over time have always been dependent on the kindness of strangers, on frequently dangerous and dark underground roads. In this book, we'll meet people who decided to turn their backs to the United States and their faces north to Canada, and then gifted Canada with their tough love and devotion. My goal is to tell these immigration and refugee stories from the ground up, and to offer brief reflections on the influences of immigration, Indigenous, defence, and other policies of the day from both countries.

The Canadian legend we especially love is that Canada has always been a haven of sanity, peace, and good government in all eras. In the more contemporary words of U2 singer Bono and former US President Barack Obama, "The world needs more Canada." *Yes*, it does. I agree. However, we like to believe the haven is always there for those fleeing the frequent political, social, racial, and cultural insanity and violence of the United States. That's not totally true. Canada will be a better country if we can look honestly at the eras and incidents when this was not the case.

The US has its own, rather different, story about these same waves of immigrants to Canada: "Those people used to be bad troublemakers, but now we forgive them." That's not completely true either. Neither the danger posed to American well-being by those fleeing to Canada nor the US declaration of forgiveness is entirely true.

Like most national mythologies, neither narrative reflects the real experiences of immigrants and refugees who have moved from the United States to Canada— whether they are the present-day descendants of Loyalists from the Revolutionary War and the War of 1812, survivors of the Underground Railroad generations later, families blacklisted by Un-American Activities Committees, supporters of the black Civil Rights movement, Vietnam War resisters, or resisters of current US wars.

While their specific circumstances vary, their stories have several important elements in common: these immigrants or refugees have left the United States for pressing reasons. Life is much better, if not perfect, in Canada, and they have tried to become the best Canadians they can be. Canada benefits from their presence here, and they don't go back to the United States once they can. The social justice antennae of the newcomers start to vibrate, though, when they detect something negative in Canada, and they then work to correct it. Sometimes they work aggressively because, after all, they are stylistically Americans! The people portrayed in this book are passionate, committed Canadians able to articulate the differences between the two countries. They also become actively worried when they see those differences disappearing.

This is not a simple story of simple paths taken. It's complicated. The reasons for fleeing the United States might have seemed simple at the time. The reasons for staying in Canada permanently are more complicated. And the reasons for being critical of both countries are more complicated yet.

The motto of the Order of Canada is *desiderantes meliorem patriam*—they desire a better country. I include this motto in my closing remarks while presiding over the citizenship ceremony. I tell the new citizens that I am eligible to preside because of membership in the order, but that this "desire [for] a better country" and the work necessary to achieve it are now the responsibility of all of us. Citizenship is a licence to desire, work for, and actively support, as needed, a better country. This same desire is a characteristic of the American refugees we meet in this book.

MY STORY: WHICH EMANCIPATION DAY?

August 1, 1945, in Houston Negro Hospital is the beginning of my story. I now immediately tell audiences in Canada my birth location because they always ask, "Where are you from?" I then hasten to add, "For the record, I have been black and a woman ever since." This includes after my immigration to Canada in 1967 as a centennial bride and since I became a Canadian citizen in 1975. You can do the math: I lived in the United States for twenty-one years, and I have lived in Canada for fifty-one years as of this writing.

Among other cultural differences, this has meant a change in Emancipation Day. For me, it will always be June 19, the day that word of President Abraham Lincoln's January 1, 1863, Emancipation Proclamation reached Texas and my slave ancestors. For Canadians who observe and remember, however, January 1, 1833, is the date of the Act of Parliament of the United Kingdom Abolishing Slavery throughout the British Empire. The date is significant because it marks the year that slavery in Canada was abolished, slavery having been largely written out of our national narrative.

The Texas Emancipation Day continues to loom in my story. Throughout this book, I quote from some of my previous work—fictionalized theatre scripts, screenplays, journalistic essays, and opinion pieces—to excavate my story as a US expat who has made Canada her permanent home. The ongoing need to analyze and understand my own migration is in all of those works.

In my one-woman play *Smoked Glass Ceiling*, I chronicle how racism, sexism, power distribution, and discrimination have evolved for me over time. Emancipation and
freedom fighting have moved from childhood in the pre–
civil rights Deep South—where it meant discrimination
in public facilities, education, and accommodation—to
mature years in the new millennium in Canada. In Canada
now, freedom fighting usually means something entirely
different for me: gender parity in governance and executive management, ethnic diversity on boards of directors,
and removing barriers to one's highest calling. Definitely
the battles are less about survival, but they are just as crucial and hard to win. Says the Rita character in *Smoked
Glass Ceiling*:

> So on the Juneteenth eve, the year 2001—like any self-
> respecting Coloured Lady of Culture and Loveliness, as
> we used to call ourselves in high school—am I barbe-
> quing a cow? Baking corn bread and peach cobbler? (not
> that I know how). Washing collard greens and making
> sure we've got enough Jack Daniels?
>
> No. I am not. I am not engaged in any of these wor-
> thy pursuits—as if I know what day it is, the 19th of June.
>
> Because what I have is a genuine emergency. A televi-
> sion regulatory, Ottawa-style emergency. On this eve of
> Emancipation Day, the day the word of master Lincoln's
> proclamation freeing the slaves got to Texas—I'm tied
> to an IV drip in an Ottawa hospital emergency room.

"An unknown infection is getting closer to your heart," says the doctor. "Good you got here in time to stop that poison."

My heart, my life at that moment and for the last 15 years, is the little TV network I helped to build.

I go to a hearing at the CRTC for Vision TV's licence renewal the next day. The IV line is still in my arm. It gets 2 more feeds. This is an attempt to put a stop to the poison that works its way to my heart, my life, my work.[4]

It was truly a long walk to freedom from a childhood of segregated schools, playgrounds, water fountains, and restrooms in 1950s Texas to middle age as a senior media executive in Canada. In 2001, that executive was trying to protect a multicultural, multifaith, non-sexist, non-homophobic, peace-affirming, not-for-profit television network from losing all of those values. The reasons that both battles are freedom fights, with winners and losers, say a great deal about the histories, politics, philosophies, and even fighting styles of the two countries.

The lives of the former US citizens whom we will meet in this book are defined by a number of complex factors. My approach in sharing their stories, therefore, is of necessity multi-faceted: in each case, I explore their reasons as individuals and as members of a group for leaving the United States, consider the differences between Canadian and American policies at the time, look at their

reasons for becoming permanent residents and then citizens of Canada given the chance to return to the United
States, and then, finally, highlight their concerns about the
policies, practices, and attitudes of their new Canadian
homeland. All of the stories in this book also shed light
on and change *my* story as a US immigrant to Canada. It's
complicated.

ONE

OPENING SNAPSHOTS
LOYAL TO WHAT
AND TO WHOM?

THE DAY AFTER

On November 9, 2016, the day after Donald J. Trump was elected president of the United States, some temporary residents of Canada had a sort of a national identity conversion experience. As one of them said to me, "This is it. We hadn't been able to make up our minds, but now we're applying for permanent residency." It seemed to be that prior to the election these folks wanted to keep their options open. They might have wanted to return to the United States for a grand employment opportunity, less expensive housing than in Canada's big cities, a warmer climate, or substantially lower taxes. The results of the 2016 election seemed to forecast, however, that these potential advantages wouldn't actually materialize. Perhaps it was much better to "commit" to Canada.

The day after the 2016 US election another Toronto resident, who'd arrived for a very good specialist job, thought it best to stay put. Plus, the dangers of living in the States, including gun crime, seem to be getting worse. The knee-jerk reaction was to remain in Canada, to hunker down.

Another long-term dual citizen decided in the evening of the 2016 US election to shed American status. No more dual. The advantage had been the possibility of working in the States from time to time. And the possibility of children and grandchildren working in the States. This advantage had seldom been exercised and didn't look as if it would come up again anytime soon. The United States was hostile to the arts and international co-ventures, whether in business, education, or science. Plus, the disadvantages had to be weighed: a conservative US government hostile to visible minorities and international travel; no end to the wars to be fought, a questionable privilege of American citizenship; and, of course, taxes to be filed even if no payment was required. The day after the election it seemed to be worth the cost and stress of shedding American citizenship.

Canada rather suddenly seemed to have a number of positive points for those who had until then remained undecided. The current Liberal government, which will most likely be in power until 2020, has affirmed its commitment to the sciences, research, and the arts. For the most part, Canadians continue to affirm and welcome refugees. The government passed a private member's bill to combat Islamophobia. And finally, then, there is Medicare, universal health coverage for all.

LOYALISTS PRO AND CON

In the classic definition, a Loyalist is one who was on the side of the British, not that of the Americans, in the Revolutionary War and the War of 1812. To claim a Loyalist history in the new millennium in Canada, however, is to dance around a number of possible contradictions in how this past history is viewed. For instance, here are a few of the competing narratives about Canada's Loyalist past:

- The Loyalists were/are a rigidly pure white/ Anglo British group.

  or

- The Loyalists were/are early adopters of multiculturalism and inclusion, especially of the despised Indigenous and black minorities prior to the abolition of slavery in the British Empire.

  or

- The Loyalists were all men, hearty, working-class stock, who had been rejected by the British class system and escaped.

  or

- The Loyalists included women, all of middle-
  class stock, who wanted to protect the British
  values that privileged them.

  or
- The Loyalists were all aristocratic Anglo men.

  or
- The Loyalists recognized the equality of women,
  and women settlers in leadership roles brought
  a very civilizing instinct to the colonies.

In his book *Inventing the Loyalists: The Ontario Loyalist Tradition and the Creation of Usable Pasts,* Norman Knowles offers an explanation of why we have come to have these contradictory narratives: "The Loyalist past was constructed and remade by various groups interested in the creation of usable pasts that spoke to present anxieties and interests." Knowles notes that "the efforts of early feminists and Native activists to appropriate the Loyalist past to their own ends highlight the important role played by gender and race in the construction of public memory."[1]

Some Loyalist descendants have less-than-proud histories. One said, "My ancestors were poor. They never moved off their one land-granted acre for generations. They were so parochial, they were afraid to travel from the ancestral township to Montreal. My ancestors worked hard at not learning French." For this person, having a Loyalist background in contemporary Canada was akin to inheriting both an impoverished and a snobbish history about which to be embarrassed. All of the reunions and getting one's name on the Loyalist registers felt like a simple pedigree grab. Yet, even in the embarrassment there was regret that the person didn't ask more questions about the ancestors, especially why the family was so timid, so frightened.

Another Loyalist descendant had a striking experience of the differences between Canada and the United States. She grew up in Canada, believing the story that there are few differences between the two countries, and then immigrated to the States in the early 2000s. She had grown up watching American television, listening to American music, and admiring the entrepreneurial spirit in the United States. A job in Washington, DC, seemed like a great opportunity, and it was time for a change.

This mature Canadian citizen, who always thought the differences between the two countries were minuscule, was overwhelmed by the culture shock she experienced. How to describe it? First, there was competition over everything, from the extremely petty to the fairly significant. To her, the American style felt totally competitive compared with the Canadian style of consensus. Second, individuals in the United States, even smart ones, believed they were independent and self-made, so there was no need for a social safety net. Third, there was in the United States a profound belief in not questioning persons in authority.

These major differences this Canadian transplant experienced while working for a US news organization finally meant she had to return home. After all, these differences in attitude create vast differences in how news is reported. We are certainly even more aware of the tensions over how news is defined since 2016. Our Canadian had to return home to values to which she was loyal: consensus, a social safety net, and the need to question authority—at least some of the time.

And, as is true for all refugees from the United States, the story evolves over time: the saga of why one fled, why one stayed in Canada after the United States forgave him or her, and what needs reaffirming or changing in Canada. For Canada, the host country, the story of why any particular group of refugees was welcomed also changes and adapts according to our contemporary national rhetoric.

ANGLO LOYALTY: THE KENNEDY CLAN
AND THE GIRTY SWORD, UPPER CANADA

Some Loyalists have argued passionately for their version of history with great pride. Patricia Kennedy's cherished account of Loyalist history is not polite, conservative, or elitist. The ancestor whom Pat most proudly claims was radical, activist, and more than inclusive of marginalized Indigenous peoples and people of colour. For those who fear siding with the despised, Pat's ancestor might be the devil incarnate.

I first heard of Pat's radical Loyalist history at an elegant wedding in Ontario. Pat is the mother of the groom and had travelled from British Columbia, where she has made her home for most of her adult life. At this wedding, the cake was proudly cut with the Girty sword, as wedding cakes in her family have been for several generations.

As Pat communicated to me in 2016, the sword was handed down from one of her ancestors, Prideaux Girty, in the War of 1812 (and not for cutting cakes):

> He was the son of Simon Girty, a famous Loyalist who was motivated to defend the interest of the Indian tribes of Western Pennsylvania and Ohio against the American Revolutionaries who wanted to take over their land by annulling the Proclamation of 1763 (the real reason for Revolution, according to some historians, including Phillip Hoffman, author of *Simon Girty, Turncoat Hero*).[2]

Pat joyfully recounted a day in her London, Ontario, high school when she had to defend the reputation of her ancestor. Young Pat could be silent no longer while Simon Girty was labelled a traitor and a scoundrel by her teacher. Pat rose to her feet and said that, to the contrary, Girty was a patriot, a Loyalist, someone who had stood up for the dispossessed. Her high school's characterization of Girty, she thought, most likely came from Stephen Vincent Benét's beloved 1936 short story "The Devil and Daniel Webster," later a popular movie and a play. In Benét's story, numerous villains considered to have betrayed the United States are named, and Girty is one of them. Webster points

to Girty in the short story and calls him a "renegade...
who saw white men burned at the stake and whooped with
the Indians to see them burn. His eyes were green, like a
catamount's, and the stains on his hunting shirt did not
come from the blood of the deer."[3] Fictional fame was all
very well, but young Pat had to set the record straight. Her
ancestor was not a traitor, no Benedict Arnold, also among
Benét's accused. Girty was a patriot, she told the class.

The story of Simon Girty is included on William R.
Wilson's website *Historical Narratives of Early Canada*.
Wilson's narrative begins with an epigraph based on pub-
licity material for Hoffmann's *Simon Girty, Turncoat Hero:*
"Simon Girty was a sharp-witted, rascally...frontiersman
whose epic adventures span the French and Indian War,
Dunmore's War, the American War for Independence, the
Indian Wars, and the War of 1812."[4] And Wilson's subti-
tle for the Girty narrative—"History's realities are seldom
dull"—is certainly an appropriate one, as we can see even
in this brief account of Girty's later life and of reactions
following his death:

> ...Feared and hated on the American frontier, Simon
> Girty eventually retired to a farm in Amherstberg,
> Upper Canada where he raised corn for the govern-
> ment. Blind, crippled and a shadow of his former self,
> he spent his happiest hours at his favorite public house
> recounting tales of his spine-tingling career. Even then a
> $1,000 American bounty remained on his head. He died

on the 18th of February, 1818. Warriors on both sides of
the Canadian border respected and remembered him
fondly. To the Mohawks, Simon Girty was to become
an **"Indian Patriot."** American frontiersmen called him
a white savage and years later, Kentuckians crossed the
Detroit River into Canada **"just for the satisfaction of
spitting on his grave."**[5] [bold in the original]

The grave-spitting story is another one about her
ancestor that Pat laughingly said her father loved to tell.
She had no way of knowing if it was true. However, true
or false, it tells us how proud the clan is of their controversial ancestor. Pat's father claimed to have actually seen
Americans cross the border into Ontario to spit on Girty's
grave. That's certainly an attention-getting claim to make.

Pat's Vietnam War resister husband, Jim, has become
the background researcher, guardian, and promoter of
her Loyalist history. He has those scholarly skills, which
he has used since crossing the border in the 1960s to
make significant contributions to environmental mining in Canada, and he has been cited as an "industry
leader...at the forefront of the mining industry's movement to sustainable development."[6] His private description of himself is that of a "late-arriving Loyalist" who
has gathered further information on the clan he joined
after crossing the border, including information about
another Loyalist ancestor, William Kennedy. This particular Kennedy, Pat says,

is one of the founders of what is now the town of Aurora
north of Toronto. Kennedy Street in Aurora runs down
the middle of the 200-acre tract that was his farm. He
was from Southern Maryland. He fought the whole
[Revolutionary] war in the Prince of Wales American
Regiment, was captured and ransomed after a couple of
years, was mustered out after the defeat at Yorktown,
confined for a while in New York City, and eventually
evacuated by the British to New Brunswick, and then
moved in 1803 to Ontario (Upper Canada), where he got
a land grant from Governor Simcoe.[7]

These are the Loyalist stories that Pat is proud to tell
her children and grandchildren, stories that affirm Canada
as a haven for the dispossessed, for Indigenous peoples, for
minorities, for strong women-led families.

Pat has had a long career teaching English as a Second
Language. This professional choice, she states, says a lot
about her relation to newcomers, to those who wish to
become Canadian, contribute to society, and seek a better life. These are family stories that Pat's Vietnam War
resister, or late-arriving Loyalist, husband has been more
than willing to adopt.

The Girty sword is being polished in preparation for
the next wedding in the Kennedy clan.

TWO

CANADIAN
LOYALTY TESTED
THE DEFENSIVE SPOTS

AFRO LOYALTY 1: CAROLYNN AND
SYLVIA WILSON, ONTARIO

The people behind the stories of immigrants and refugees from the United States to Canada are never quite whom I expect them to be. We are living through a moment when the diversity of the stories, and the nature of the backstories, might surprise many long-term Canadians. For instance, as we look further at one of the oldest waves of refugees, the Loyalists, who would have expected so many black people?

I was surprised to learn recently of a former American refugee settlement of black people close to my home of almost twenty-five years in Horseshoe Valley, Ontario, in the Township of Oro-Medonte. The mysterious settlement was tied to the War of 1812, but by the early 1900s the inhabitants were gone. Where? Why?

At least one theory is that these were black soldiers' families given land grants to protect a northern water route from Toronto to Lake Simcoe. In a sparsely inhabited Simcoe county, it's possible these families were a line of defence against the Americans and were being rewarded for service in the War of 1812. Another speculation is that they were escaped slaves who arrived in the north country via the Underground Railroad. What I discovered was that some of the descendants of this mysterious black community, farther north than one typically thinks of the Underground Railroad running, maintain cohesive forms of activism and community involvement.

On a beautiful summer day in 2016, I drove an hour south of my home, just a bit beyond the resort town of Collingwood on Nottawasaga Bay at the southern point of Georgian Bay. In the village of Clarksburg, the signature blue Ontario historic site sign beckons: "Sheffield Park Black History and Cultural Museum." Deep curiosity about what happened to this sizable black community in the 1800s is what took me to the museum. The family who runs it is related to families from Oro, Collingwood, and Owen Sound. These refugees and their descendants stayed in the north. They didn't go to the less isolated southern locations of Toronto, Chatham, London, and Niagara, or back to the United States when it was safer to do so. They were and are at home in the north.

These black communities were small in the 1700s, 1800s, and 1900s, and they remain small now. They are small groups in small towns. Perhaps, after the Fugitive Slave Act was passed by Congress in 1850, freedom seekers in these northern, hard-to-travel-to, thinly populated villages were harder to track down. Perhaps it wasn't even worthwhile financially to search for them.

Descendants of those early black refugees are active community members in the Collingwood area, specifically with their Heritage Community Church and the Sheffield Park Black History and Cultural Museum. I was invited by the dynamos behind the museum, sisters Sylvia and Carolynn Wilson, for a picnic on Sunday afternoon in a screened gazebo on the museum grounds. Twenty minutes late, having made a wrong turn, I was out of breath and apologizing profusely. Carolynn said with great warmth and a smile, "Relax, you're at home now." And she meant it. Since I'm a black woman who found them from my birthplace in Texas to their Collingwood home, I was embraced. The sisters' achievements are staggering: an eleven-acre museum site with displays housed in a dozen buildings, representing the preservation and growth of a small initiative started by their deceased uncle, Howard Sheffield, and financed by the two sisters, their elderly

mother, and their friends. Plus, their Heritage Community
Church, still a working church, is their anchor, originally a
black congregation when worship was segregated, but now
welcoming and including all.

*Sylvia Wilson (left) and Carolynn Wilson (right) (Wilson
family photos)*

It is evident that Carolynn and Sylvia have learned
many lessons from their remarkable ancestors, whom they
cherish. The following note about their Uncle Howard is
from a nearby Presbyterian church's bulletin in 2013:

It was the dream of Collingwood resident Howard
Sheffield to gather and preserve the history of his ancestors to share with his family. He wanted to keep the
events of the past visible so we, and future generations,
would never forget. Howard's dream lives on at Sheffield
Park Black History and Cultural Museum.[1]

Persistence, resilience, and "this is our home too" are
lessons that these black descendants of refugees from the
War of 1812, or travellers on the Underground Railroad, or
fugitive slaves, have thoroughly learned.

Another of Carolynn and Sylvia's ancestors, their Uncle
Wilfred, was chronicled by Judy Plaxton in the *Globe and
Mail's* "Lives Lived" column of May 15, 2015. Wilfred
Sheffield had been active in sports and on student council
in high school, and graduated with honours. He went on
to work in a foundry, and he served in the Second World
War. After the war, he earned his Theology degree and was
ordained as a Baptist minister in 1952, something he had
wanted "from as far back as I can remember." In his first
parish in Burk's Falls, Ontario, he was known as "the first
black minister of an all-white church." Plaxton recounts a
favourite family story from his time at Burk's Falls:

One day, as [Reverend Wilfred] walked along the street,
a police car pulled up and the officer called out, "Come
over here." Wilfred got into the car while the officer con-
tacted his department. "Make sure you haven't got the

Baptist minister," came the response, and Wilfred spoke up, saying, "I am he." He and the officer later became friends and often had coffee together.

Plaxton's tribute is an accurate and moving account of the northern Ontario backdrop as experienced by black people, and she notes, "In his quiet, determined way, Wilfred was a symbol of courage and commitment in working to break down the racial barriers he faced."[2]

Wilfred's way of life, as lived, characterizes Sylvia and Carolynn's way of coping with their sometimes racist world. During my visit, their other role model snoozed quietly in the gazebo while we had lunch. Mother Yvonne Sheffield Wilson, ninety-three, dozed that Sunday afternoon, but Carolynn said, "She knows we're here, and she can see us."

In one of the museum's impressive displays there is a clipping of Yvonne's achievements as a high school student in the 1930s. In 1932, Yvonne was track and field champion of Collingwood Collegiate Institute, yet she wasn't permitted to go on to the regional competition. Although we can speculate now about the reasons, Mrs. Wilson has advanced no theory. Was it that no one would billet a black student at the regionals in Orillia? Was it that she couldn't be sent outside as the face of Collingwood?

The family museum recognizes Yvonne's athletic accomplishments. And a white friend suggested to the high school that Yvonne be recognized for those accomplishments regardless of how many years later. Therefore, in 2008, she was inducted into the Black and Gold Society of Collingwood Collegiate Institute. The society recognized Yvonne Sheffield Wilson's "outstanding athletic achievement" of seventy-six years earlier.

Carolynn and Sylvia have put their arms around the memories and histories of the remaining black community. They remember elders who did not survive as well as their mother and uncles. They remember an elderly black woman afraid to go out of her house in Collingwood. She was afraid of her white neighbours. Her husband went to live in a senior citizens home upon her death but would not be cared for by white people. The sisters never knew exactly the reasons, but they did know that as youngsters they had to take food to this fearful family.

Carolynn and Sylvia seem to have boundless energy and determination. Imagine setting up a respectable, medium-sized local history museum with your own labour and finances. In a 2010 interview Carolynn spoke about how respect for their family and community history inspires their work:

> It also gives us energy and encouragement that we are loved and that we are respected, that we did contribute. We weren't just left behind. We're a somebody, and we can go forward....So there's the issue of self-esteem. [...] Our grandfather often said that he looked around and [asked], "Why aren't there more Black people in

business?" He'd ask, "Why not?"…[W]hen we looked back in our history for those who travelled to Grey County and are buried in that cemetery, they had skills of barn building and other skills of teaching, and so forth. So we can say we have those skills that they have. And so we go forward, if we can.[3]

■ ■ ■

In 2015 to 2016, in the Township of Oro-Medonte, another part of the northern communities Sylvia and Carolynn define as home, there was a flurry of activity to restore an historic black church just fifteen minutes from my house. Generous fundraising made this restoration possible, and local building trades contributed material and labour. Summer perfection characterized August 19, 2016, when hundreds of people gathered under tents and sat on hay bales to cheer the restoration of the Oro African Church. The small structure will now stand proudly for another 100 years at least. The township's news release invited us all: "With the preservation project nearly complete, the re-opening of the church celebrates the strength of diversities of culture, religion and race in the way that our Nation came together to save the church."[4]

Ceremony and celebrity reigned at the restoration ceremony: a breathtaking three-plane flyover of Second World War aircraft to salute the church; elderly gentlemen re-enactors in red uniforms from the War of 1812; the chief and eagle staff carriers from the Rama First Nation; the Honourable Elizabeth Dowdeswell, twenty-ninth lieutenant-governor of Ontario, who brought greetings from Her Majesty Queen Elizabeth II; and the master of ceremonies, Michael Lutrell "Pinball" Clemons, a player with the Toronto Argonauts of the Canadian Football League for twelve seasons and twice their head coach. Celebration and celebrity don't get much better than that! The primary organizer behind the fundraising and restoration, much-honoured Janie Cooper-Wilson, wept with thanksgiving. Her great-great-grandparents, Charlie Thomas and Jane Montgomery, had been married in the African Methodist Episcopal Church in 1864.

But the significance of this site is about more than family history. The church was built in the 1840s—"one of the oldest such African log structures still standing in North America"—and has been designated a National Historic Site. A plaque on the site "pays tribute to Runchey's Coloured Corps, an all-black militia unit that fought for Britain in the War of 1812," a nod to the fact that this structure is "one of the few remaining links to a period in Canadian history where blacks fought side by side with whites for a common cause." For Cooper-Wilson, the restoration project was about bringing "the community together, to right the wrongs of the past."[5]

At the star-studded reopening, I talked to one of the many descendants who sat in reserved seats. This attractive older woman with light-brown skin had come from

Alberta for the event. She didn't know why her ancestors
had moved away from Oro-Medonte in the 1800s, but she
had a book of photographs of all those whom she had been
able to trace. The rainbow of skin colours in the photos
was impressive, from dark ebony to pale white. Said the
Albertan, "Of course, some family members aren't in my
book. They didn't want it known they had a touch of tar."

*Ribbon Cutting, Oro African Church, 2016 (Courtesy of
Oro-Medonte Township)*

The summer of 2016 also featured an exhibition, *If These
Walls Could Talk*, in the Orillia History Museum about the
black community in Oro-Medonte in the 1800s. There are
proud descendants who no longer live in the township but
are eager to make their ancestors' lives known to people

today. The curator of the exhibition, John Merritt, has made this disappearing black community the subject of his extremely insightful MA thesis, "Remembering the Past, Legitimizing the Present: The Campaigns to Preserve the African Methodist Episcopal Church in Oro Township in Canadian Social Memory in the 1940s and the Present Day."

As Merritt explains,

> between 1819 and 1831, the government of Upper Canada used preferential policies to grant Crown land in Oro Township, which at the time was on the northern frontier of the province, to black Upper Canadians. Initially, when black Upper Canadians…petitioned the government for free Crown land, they were only granted land in Oro Township, unlike white Upper Canadians, who could usually pick and choose from anywhere in the province where they wanted their grants to be. However, at the same time, black people who had been born in the United States were usually granted land, unlike white American immigrants, who were refused the privileges associated with British citizenship. After 1825, when free grants of land were restricted to military veterans and descendants of United Empire Loyalists, black Upper Canadians were able to purchase land in Oro Township at a 75% discount (1 shilling an acre). In both cases, African-Canadian grantees received half the amount of land as white settlers in Oro Township (100 vs. 200 acres).[6]

It seems impossible now to discover where members of the community went after settling initially in Oro-Medonte. Were they driven out by racism? Was the land too difficult to farm? Were living wages elsewhere more attractive? Merritt offers some possibilities:

> During this period, about sixty black Upper Canadians were granted land in Oro Township, but only about half of these actually settled there, or stayed there for any appreciable amount of time: a proportion which was probably similar among white pioneers, due to the hardship of pioneer life and the common practice of pioneers selling their deeds to land speculators. Unlike some of their white neighbours, none of the African-Canadian settlers of Oro Township appear[s] to have established successful businesses or farms. This may have been because most of the land they were located on by the government was of poor quality (this probably wouldn't have been intentional, since government agents usually could only guess about the fertility of virgin land)....The African-Canadian settlers appear to have mostly worked as waged labourers, mostly for neighbouring (white) farmers. Unfortunately, a lot of the details about the lives these people led in Oro are not available, because they left no journals or letters and [because] references to them in the writings of their white neighbours are quite fleeting.[7]

What we do know is that the community was there, since the shell of the church remains as evidence. What we also know is that the government of the day, just this once, made homesteads available to black citizens. The Loyalist promises made but then broken in Nova Scotia during the Revolutionary War and the War of 1812 were kept for a moment in one Ontario township. Merritt isn't certain why:

> We essentially have to guess about why the government chose to settle these people specifically in Oro Township, since there is no surviving official explanation for this policy. Although the African-Canadian settlers...have since been remembered either as fugitive African-American slaves from the Underground Railroad or as veterans of Runchey's Coloured Corps (an all-black Canadian militia regiment that fought during the War of 1812), neither of these descriptions accurately describes all of the settlers; but both descriptions do apply to some of them....Most of those who left Oro moved to nearby cities such as Barrie, Collingwood, and Toronto, where there were more opportunities for waged labour; others moved to the United States. By 1900 or so, there were only about five African-Canadian families still living in the township.[8]

The black inhabitants of Oro-Medonte are gone, but their small church still stands. Meanwhile, the history-

preserving ancestors of Sylvia and Carolynn Wilson in
Collingwood held on to jobs, businesses, land, and their
church.

Merritt concludes that each era has had a favoured narrative of the history of the black settlers:

> For decades, the local white community had remem-
> bered the African-Canadian settlers of Oro Township
> (probably by virtue of their skin colour) as fugitive slaves
> who had travelled there from the United States via the
> Underground Railroad....
>
> In the 1970s, new research by local historians W. A.
> Fisher and Gary French revealed that at least some (if
> not most) of the African-Canadian settlers had not in
> fact been escaped slaves, but either free immigrants from
> the northern United States or citizens of Upper Canada.
> Fisher and French suggested that the African-Canadian
> War of 1812 veterans might have been settled in Oro to
> defend the road (now Highway 93) between the naval
> base at Penetanguishene and the route to Toronto via
> Lake Simcoe and Yonge Street from a future American
> invasion (in 1814 American warships had briefly seized
> control of Lake Huron). In light of this new evidence, the
> regular services at the AME church site began to remem-
> ber the African-Canadian settlement in Oro Township
> as part of Canada's multicultural history rather than part
> of the Underground Railroad legend.[9]

Merritt makes a compelling case for the mood of the times determining the best story about where the black community came from, disappeared to, and why. It does seem, without any dishonesty or manipulation, that different narratives of the same events are more politically and socially compelling in different eras:

> The accounts of these campaigns, and the popular histories of Canada's relationship with race which they represented, ignored Canada's own history of black slavery….Both campaigns, in characterizing Canada as moral, progressive, tolerant, and equitable to racial minorities since the phasing out of slavery in the province in the 1790s, also ignore a far longer heritage on the part of mainstream Canadian society of immoral, regressive, intolerant, and unfair treatment of minorities, beginning with the First Nations.[10]

There isn't one tidy reason why these black American immigrants, refugees, fugitives, or freedom seekers crossed the border into Canada. Nor is there one tidy reason why they stayed in Canada or one succinct account of the challenges they faced and the opportunities they found. However, given many shades of grey, Canada seemed to them a more just society than the United States. That might be what we want to hear, that Canada is a more just society, but it is only part of the truth.

We are left, in the words of Sylvia Hamilton, whom we'll meet in the next section, with "parallel narratives."

We could say, on the one hand, that whatever works to sustain a positive social/political purpose is good. On the other, our favourite stories frequently serve to keep the truth from us. Whether knowingly or unknowingly, we lie to ourselves, and this isn't a healthy habit.

Those pillars of Collingwood, Sylvia and Carolynn, remember their father, who was light-skinned and worked for the City of Collingwood in a mid-level supervisory capacity, suddenly making an early trip home one day at lunch time. He was almost covered in tar. He had to clean himself up. Some of his fellow workers had thought it would be amusing to tar him. Mr. Wilson needed to remove the tar, maintain his dignity somehow, and return to work as soon as possible, as if nothing had happened. The incident was never discussed with his young daughters, though they have long remembered it. In 2017, a television journalism piece was produced on his sudden death in 1955. While working on a cherry picker and in the employ of the city, he crashed to the pavement and was killed. There was no explanation beyond "accident" at the time, no investigation, and no compensation for his widow with her two young children.[11] Being able to talk about the tar incident and finally the death of their father seems to set the sisters free. As Sylvia and Carolynn Wilson state, "This is our home. We don't give up. We hang on as long as we can."[12]

▌ ▌ ▌

When I got to the funeral home, a large, remodelled, elegant old house, there was standing room only for the service for Yvonne Sheffield Wilson, who passed away at the age of ninety-five on November 23, 2016. It was impossible to get a glimpse into the main room where the family and clergy were seated. Members of Mother Wilson's lodge, for the most part very elderly ladies, feelingly eulogized her. Their themes were that, whatever happened to Yvonne, wrongs and prejudices, or gifts and compliments, she was always a lady, beautiful, gracious, and faithful to her family, friends, and church. The entire population of Collingwood seemed to be there, regardless of colour, as well as a rainbow of people from everywhere in Ontario. The weather was picturesque Ontario fall, maple leaf–carpeted, warm, ideal for telling stories of someone who'd been in the community for ninety-five years. The crowd at the funeral, the burial at the cemetery, and the reception afterward at the church were the perfect picture of a Canadian small-town community: black, white, and *café au lait* skin colours; young and old; accents from central Canada, the West Indies, and Europe. The family was recognized for making significant contributions to the community: a restaurant, a church, a museum, and the labour of generations.

The Sheffield Wilsons have passed every test of loyalty to Canada. Has Canada been loyal to them? Not always. I've recounted three unfortunate incidents in which the family was betrayed by their home territory:

Yvonne Sheffield as a young athlete not being able to travel
with her high school's winning team; a tar episode in
Collingwood; and the uninvestigated, non-compensated
death of Herbert Wilson, a young father, while working for
the city. Throughout it all, the sisters have remained loyal
to their home, which they love and to which they contribute, and they are not moving.

AFRO LOYALTY 2:
SYLVIA D. HAMILTON, NOVA SCOTIA

Black Loyalists have the same pride in themselves and
their ancestors as do conservative or politically radical
Anglo Loyalists. The same love for Canada and the same
fierce desire to make a better country are there too, despite
how badly these black immigrants and their descendants
have often been treated.

Sylvia Hamilton, an internationally respected, award-
winning black filmmaker[13] whose ancestors arrived as
Loyalists during the War of 1812, has one defiant answer
to the question "Where are you from?" That is the question that causes many people of colour, including me, to
run metaphorically screaming from the room. Hamilton's
answer—"Nova Scotia"—is stated proudly, firmly, and
confidently. The questioner then often asks, "Before that?"
Again, "Nova Scotia" is her assured answer.

Sylvia had the opportunity to share stories about her
family's Loyalist history during a conversation about her

book of poetry *And I Alone Escaped to Tell You* with the dynamic and insightful Shelagh Rogers in 2016 on CBC Radio's *The Next Chapter*:

> The people, especially in the early pages, came to me out of history. There are African people who were enslaved in Nova Scotia, and there were people who were part of the black loyalist migration after the American

Sylvia D. Hamilton (University of King's College faculty photo)

Revolutionary War. Then there were people who came
to Nova Scotia after the War of 1812. They were known as
the black refugees and, indeed, my ancestors....

The Hamiltons came as part of the black refugee
migration after the War of 1812. They had been enslaved
on plantations in St. Simons Island in Georgia and had
escaped when Britain offered freedom to any enslaved
person who would fight with the British. So they got
themselves off that plantation somehow and made their
way behind British lines and, after the end of that war,
made their way to New York and arrived in Nova Scotia
on these tall transport ships.[14]

Both Sylvia and I were honoured to be asked to write
essays for the Aboriginal Healing Foundation to be
included in the book *Cultivating Canada: Reconciliation
through the Lens of Cultural Diversity*, the third volume
of the foundation's research series. The first two volumes
were authored primarily by Indigenous people about the
legacies, memories, and personal and national learnings
from residential schools. Our volume contained essays
from fairly recent immigrants about their relationships
with Indigenous peoples. In Sylvia's case, fairly recent is
since the War of 1812, more than 200 years and ten generations ago. In my case, fairly recent is since 1967, when
I became a first-generation immigrant to Canada. Sylvia
wrote about the "little black school houses" in Nova Scotia
and Ontario for the Aboriginal Healing Foundation book.

I have to admit, with some embarrassment, that I was profoundly shocked and shaken when I first saw Sylvia's *The Little Black School House* film. Why? Because, as a black person who grew up in the American South, the story I knew about Canada was that, as soon as slaves or the descendants of slaves crossed the border, they were free at last! Immigrating myself in Canada's proud centennial year to southwestern Ontario, where there were major terminals of the Underground Railroad, I believed 100 percent that this freedom story had miraculously happened to me. In fact, I was rather smug telling friends and family members in Texas that I had immigrated to the most enlightened country in the world. Consequently, I didn't like Sister Hamilton telling me in her film, some forty years later when I was in my sixties, that the schools in Nova Scotia had been segregated as long as the schools I'd attended in Texas. Moreover, she rubbed it in: there had been segregated schools in southwestern Ontario not far from where I made my first Canadian home. This wasn't good news, and as a well-educated person I was embarrassed not to know this history, now my Canadian history. That is the power of the Canada-and-black-people narrative that both Canadians and Americans tell themselves. The Underground Railroad was of course gloriously true for some black people, some escaped slaves, some of the time.

But it is important to tell and understand other Canadian narratives because only then can we meaningfully work toward creating the best country in the world.

Sylvia makes a huge contribution to truth-telling in her *Cultivating Canada* essay, entitled "Stories from *The Little Black School House*":

> What is not widely known or remembered is that in two Canadian provinces, because of their race, a large number of African Canadian children were also required by law to attend separate, segregated schools.
>
> Legal scholar Constance Backhouse explains that from the middle of the nineteenth century, Black and white students could be separated by law. Legislation in both Nova Scotia and Ontario allowed this division....
>
> Within Black communities throughout Canada, education has always been constructed as society's passport to a better life....
>
> The desire for education on the part of African Canadians over time was matched by the equal desire of some Canadians to keep the races apart. For example, in 1843, even though Black parents in Hamilton, Ontario, had paid taxes, they were barred from sending their children to public schools. They petitioned Governor-General Lord Elgin after receiving little help from the local officials and eventually won their rights. Yet in the same region, Amherstburg parents were less successful....
>
> I am interested [in] two questions: first, what memories have we failed to represent, and second, what memories do we not want to represent and why? The

enslavement of African-descended people in Canada sits at the cusp of these troubling questions....

Talking about slavery in Canada has been taboo. The generalized narrative asserts that African-descended people arrived in Canada via the Underground Railroad.[15]

Sylvia describes a good deal of her work as telling "parallel narratives." In many respects, *American Refugees* is also about telling parallel, or alternative, narratives about immigrants and refugees from the United States to Canada. In Canada, there are certainly times when, and places where, refugees are welcomed with open arms. Maybe not every person in the country welcomes refugees, but enough do that it becomes part of our national narrative. Those are the glorious stories that we remember and tell each other.

However, for all of the individuals portrayed in this book, there are parallel narratives: the border closes right behind them and soon does not admit others like them, or does not admit others of a different colour, or the newcomers dig deeply into the ongoing shameful treatment of Indigenous peoples in Canada and make that their issue. As long as we forget or ignore these other narratives, which cast long shadows on the glorious story of Canadian tolerance and acceptance, we give up another chance to make Canada a much better society. Sylvia's career can be characterized by the telling of these profound, sometimes shocking, parallel narratives.

I've had two particularly iconic experiences that reveal how we Canadians suppress alternative stories. My first such experience occurred in the mid-1980s at Dalhousie University in Halifax. A group of academics and community leaders gathered to brainstorm how to get the university's proposed Chair of Black Canadian Studies financed and launched. I was on the faculty of the University of Regina's School of Journalism at that time and was included in the group consulted. After much discussion about the problems in and the barriers to establishing the (black) chair, in a very impressive room with wood panels and leaded glass windows, along with portraits of (white) men in academic gowns lining the walls, I asked a question: "How many black professors are there at Dal?" I didn't think this was a challenging question; I just wanted to know on what home base the university would be building. After many moments of silence, the answer came from senior administrators: "None." I was astonished. The university had been able to gather at least a score of us, black university professors, from other parts of Canada. Yet the part of our country where the largest and oldest black population is located had not produced one doctored and tenured black professor at a great university.

It was a profound lesson in the systemic racial discrimination of the education system in Atlantic Canada that, granted, establishment of the chair would attempt to correct. I use this example in teaching university classes when I want students to understand the difference between the racist behaviour of individuals and systemic/prolonged racism.

Thankfully, the James R. Robinson Chair in Black Canadian Studies *was* established in 1991, and the incumbent is a tenured professor who, when the term is up, joins a department at Dalhousie University. This corrective to an old system of historical segregation is welcomed, but it has taken a long time.

My second iconic experience of how we rewrite our history in Canada happened in Toronto in 1994. I was invited, along with other media executives, to a prestigious private girls' school to do some media awareness work. The visit, as it happened, was during February, Black History Month. Displaying that week's TV guides from two major Toronto newspapers, I noted that one guide featured a series about the Underground Railroad, and the other featured the *Hymn to Freedom* series by Almeta Speaks about slavery in Canada as well as other historical content. This statement, which I thought was merely descriptive, caused a near riot in the audience of fifteen-year-old girls, who assured me that "There was no slavery in Canada!" They hadn't learned about slavery in their Canadian studies, in their fine school, so it didn't exist. I was somewhat shaken by this demonstration of how much we want to believe in the Underground Railroad and that coming to Canada was an unproblematic solution to American slavery and racism. Systemic discrimination in education and slavery in Canada are two alternative narratives that we strongly resist.

Sylvia Hamilton's work serves to counter this resistance. She writes: "For many generations, we have learned nothing of Canada's history of all-Black schools, segregated by law and geography in Ontario and Nova Scotia, two provinces with long-standing, historic populations of African-descended people. I consider the…extant former schoolhouses as *sites of memory*; there are generations of invisible stories embedded in these geographic sites and in the memories of the students, teachers, parents, and trustees who were the schools' communities."[16] I would argue that Hamilton's documentary work is a site of memory. So is her poetry. So was her visual arts exhibition—*Excavation: A Site of Memory*—mounted in Nova Scotia at the Dalhousie University Art Gallery in 2013 and the Maritime Museum of the Atlantic in 2014, and at the Thames Art Gallery in Chatham, Ontario, in 2015. Pamela Edmonds, a visual and media arts curator currently based in Toronto, whose focus has been on thematic exhibitions that explore the politics of representation particularly as they relate to issues of race, gender, and national identity, describes Sylvia's arts practice: "Hamilton's work gives voice to the stories of individuals silenced by racism and colonialism; she does not speak for them, but finds ways to bring these individuals forward to speak for themselves.…Here the resiliency of the African spirit is a testimony to endurance, adaptation and the ability to evolve while embarking on continual processes of imaginative recovery."[17]

This brings us back to Sylvia Hamilton the person, a descendant of refugees to Canada, black people, from the War of 1812. Yes, there are such people, though they were little noticed in Canada's expensive and noisy commemorations of that war in 2012. The narratives of black Loyalists were almost invisible. Not so in Sylvia's work: "*Excavation* visualizes the tangible markings of the enslavement of African people in Nova Scotia, through archival newspaper ads juxtaposed with photographic images, imagined poetic narratives, and everyday physical objects...."[18] It is significant that *Excavation* was seen in Nova Scotia and in southwestern Ontario, the two places where we appear to have the biggest vested interest in saying that all black people arrived in Canada via the Underground Railroad and that Canada was "the promised land" for them. I am gratified that Sylvia calls her ancestors "refugees." Yes, they had reason to flee. Yes, they had a well-founded fear of continued persecution. But, no, Canada was not a land flowing with milk and honey. As Sylvia explained in her talk on November 6, 2014, about *Excavation* at the Maritime Museum of the Atlantic in Halifax:

My ancestors, the Black Refugees, were people with emotions, feelings, imagination and great ingenuity. They had to be, had to be ingenious in order to survive. They had agency, a sense of themselves, and something beyond themselves. They shared this with other early Africans in Nova Scotia, those enslaved, the Freedom

Runners as I prefer to call them, the Black Loyalists and
the Maroons from Jamaica.

This installation stands in opposition to the pater-
nalism and racism that tried to shape their experiences.
It stands in opposition to the language used to describe
African people. I remind myself: *they were not the language.* They were people.

There were efforts to erase us, to pretend we did not
exist. That we did not count. Everything that I learned
growing up, that I learned in community and that I've
seen since has challenged this idea, actively resisted this
idea. My life's work, and this installation as part of it, has
been a way to talk back to that absence in the historical
record: to say we are here, we were here, we are here.

And I am here, because they were.

I recall the first experience of going to the Nova
Scotia Archives in [the] mid-1970s....

I remember reading old original copies of the AUBA
[African United Baptist Association] minutes from the
late 1800s into the 1900s and being struck by the detail
and the information they contained—a picture, a landscape of Black communities. It felt as if I was actually
touching my history. Up to that point, in schools and
even university, I had little…if anything about me.[19]

I talked with Sylvia in Halifax in 2015 about why I didn't
know all this. We are better off knowing these truths,
she said. All of us, of all colours, are better off knowing

them. It is the truth that will set us free. Sylvia is a marvellous guide, even for a black person like me, embarrassed by what I don't know about Canadian history. She is a non-judgmental, gentle, and graceful guide who seems to believe that it is never too late for any of us to face the truth. None of us is too old, too young, too bigoted, or too embarrassed to learn.

Her patience with all of us as we explore and learn with her is wonderful to experience. At York University's Canadian Writers in Person course, Sylvia read from her book of poetry *And I Alone Escaped to Tell You*. One participant who heard and reviewed the lecture noted that Sylvia spoke of being surprised at the "attempted erasure, and in some cases denial, of history in favor of something more palatable to the general understanding of Canadian history," including the denial of her own experience of attending a segregated school in Nova Scotia, much as the realities of residential schools were denied. The reviewer also noted that she "rankles when some people question her Nova Scotia heritage, as if she couldn't be 'from there' because she doesn't look like what 'from there' is supposed to be. Yet Hamilton and her ancestors have been there as long as anyone, and belong in a way that can't be denied."[20]

One Nova Scotia reviewer has suggested that perhaps it wasn't appropriate for him to comment on the "incendiary poetry" in *And I Alone Escaped to Tell You*, since he was white, privileged, and approaching his sixties. But he *did* comment, because he didn't want the readers of his blog to

miss out on what Sylvia Hamilton has to teach us; he calls
her poems in this volume "a sad litany, a terrible history
and a necessary part of our tapestry" and he challenges the
reader: "If some of these poems are hard to read—imagine
how hard they were to write—imagine how hard they were
to live."[21] "Melville Island" is an example of one of these
hard-to-read, hard-to-write, hard-to-live poems:

Melville Island

1814
Silenced by the snow
they wondered if even God
had finally forsaken them

home a stone prison
temporary officials say
we used to temporary

come in from the fields one day
to find out we been up and sold
we invented temporary

when they line us up
after they drag us
off them waterbeds of death
we ready for a new kind of temporary

nova scarcity
seed potatoes turnip tobacco
good crop in the fall
now all froze to the floor

and if we still here
in spring
we try again[22]

Sylvia Hamilton is patient with all of us. We're all
learning other stories that are true and therefore freeing.
In Sylvia's films, poems, and essays, we meet real black
people who were not just numbers, certainly not passive
numbers, who accepted their fate. One of her missions is
to give voice to resisters. Her refugees are not silent. They
do not give in, they do not give up, until they absolutely
have to abandon the cause. Chronicled in *And I Alone
Escaped to Tell You* and in Sylvia's exhibitions, speeches,
and conversations is a dynamic example of resistance:
Mary Postell. Postell was "a free Black Loyalist in Nova
Scotia who went to court twice to fight for her freedom
in 1785–86; she lost both times and was eventually re-en-
slaved and sold by Samuel Grey to William Mangrum
for one hundred pounds of potatoes, valued at twenty
pounds."[23] But Mary went to court twice. The point is not
that she lost twice but how actively she resisted the system
of slavery. Sylvia frequently cites Mary, and she gives us
accounts of other Loyalists, those whom we seldom meet.

These black Loyalists, ancestors of hers, are a significant part of the story of refugees from the United States to Canada. Their treatment, experiences, and activism in the generations that followed also comprise a major part of the seldom-told Canadian story.

For the Loyalists in this book, yes, Canada is a better country than the United States. Moreover, when we can tell the authentic stories of why Simon Girty impersonated an Indigenous person, what really happened to the black Loyalists, and the realities of Canada's history of slavery and segregated schools, then we can move toward being a much better country, perhaps the best.

The black Loyalists of Nova Scotia may yet obtain title to the land their families have lived on for 200 years. The province has promised money to research and finalize title on the land grant property, for which five historical black communities have paid taxes, even though they have never owned the land.[24]

AFRO LOYALTY 3:
THE MAYES FAMILY, SASKATCHEWAN

That there are any black people at all on the prairies is a miracle. When the Canadian government discovered that people of colour were answering the call to homestead in the west, it took immediate action to stop a feared invasion of black people seeking free black dirt.[25] The Mayes family, however, was not discouraged, despite the government propaganda and physical hardship, and has now been in Saskatchewan for five generations.

The early generations of the Mayes family, like many Saskatchewan pioneers, endured poverty, hunger, deep-freeze winters, and isolation. The schools were for black children only until white settlers moved in, and then the children were mixed. Many members of the Mayes family have planted deep roots, remained, excelled, and made endless contributions to Saskatchewan and Canada. Dr. Charlotte Mayes Williams is the fourth generation to thrive in rural Saskatchewan and identify its landscape as home.

Charlotte and her whole family know the history. In the early twentieth century, the Canadian government had numerous policies to discourage immigrants of colour, any colour, whether they were Asian, Jewish, West Indian, or Afro-American. And, an unfortunate surprise for immigration officials, many arrived from Commonwealth countries, which gave them a prior claim to being welcomed in Canada. However, the arrival of hundreds of black people in western Canada between 1910 and 1912 from the non-Commonwealth United States was an outrage. The government sent black spokespersons south to say how awful it would be to live in Canada and published ads to dissuade black immigrants. These tactics didn't work 100 percent. After all, if slavery and non-existent human rights were the alternatives, what was so terrible about cold weather and a bit of prejudice? Finally the federal government attempted

to implement a ban, deeming black immigrants "unsuitable." This tactic also didn't work, primarily because the
ban didn't become legislation.[26]

The Mayes family knows all of that history, yet like
Matriarch Mattie Mayes, respected midwife in the
Maidstone area, many of them have grown and flourished close to where they were planted. In the 1980s, the
Saskatchewan Archives audiotaped some thirty descendants of the original black settlers. This is how that collection is described:

> Although Canadian immigration policy did not pub-
> licly exclude black settlers, they were not welcomed.
> Canadian immigration agents in the United States were
> instructed to discourage blacks from emigrating north.
> As a result, in the period 1896 to 1907, when 1.3 million
> Europeans and American Europeans entered Canada,
> only nine hundred blacks became Canadian immi-
> grants. By 1911 the population of blacks in the prairies
> barely reached fifteen hundred. The largest black settle-
> ment in Saskatchewan was established in 1908–1909 in
> the parkland area north of Maidstone.[27]

When Rex and I moved to Saskatchewan in 1971, one of
my great-uncles in Houston mentioned rather casually that
he had answered the call for homesteaders on the Prairies
in 1910. He appeared to find it somewhat humorous that
my young family had landed there to live and work.

At this time, sixty years after his terminated homestead venture, tall and handsome Great-Uncle Ennis Powell was a dining car porter in Texas. He expressed no regret that as a young man he had returned to the warmth of Texas and family; the Prairies were "too cold, too far, and too lonely." Smugly I thought I was much hardier, and there seemed to be much opportunity available to me in Saskatchewan. I obviously had no concept of what those black settlers from Oklahoma and Texas faced in 1910. I was also looking through rose-coloured glasses at what their descendants continued to face. Youthful optimism (or stupidity) caused me not to ask Great-Uncle Ennis about what he and others actually encountered in Saskatchewan. Therefore, I do not know the truth of my great-uncle's return to the deeply racist and segregated American South.

Charlotte Mayes Williams has many reasons why she has not gone to larger Canadian centres or to the United States. Her life and distinguished work are in Elrose. Her home and business, the Hooves and Paws Veterinary Clinic, are three hours south of Maidstone. The population of Maidstone is currently listed as 1,200. Elrose is much smaller, with 477 people, but its first and only veterinarian has a much bigger area in the Coteau Hills to cover.

In December 2017, when I talked to Charlotte, she and her father, Murray Mayes, had just returned from the 100th anniversary celebration for Milleton Hall, six and a half kilometres southwest of the Mayes homestead and twenty-eight kilometres north of Maidstone. She said all the local people were delighted to see her dad, and she heard lots of stories about her father and grandfather. There were skits on the history of the hall. Charlotte became very aware of how much her ancestors were respected and valued in Maidstone.

Because there wasn't enough income on the farm to support him, as a young man Murray had moved from near Maidstone to North Battleford. There he met his wife Linda (they later divorced), and their seven children were born and grew up in North Battleford. However, Murray still owns land near Maidstone, and he and his former wife, their adult children, and extended family meet every Christmas. Charlotte says the family "will never get rid of" that land. She laughingly says that her dad "drummed into" them that if they keep their land "we will always have a place to go to if we need it."[28]

For black immigrants from Texas and Oklahoma in 1910, one place to escape to was Canada. Not that everything was perfect here, far from it. Not that they were always welcomed here, sometimes far from it. In addition to federal government actions attempting to ban the immigration of black people when (white) settlers were called for, Saskatchewan in particular experienced a flourishing of the Ku Klux Klan in the 1920s. Charlotte is familiar with the sometimes hostile reception of her ancestors. She has read *Deemed Unsuitable*, R. Bruce Shepard's 1997 book about the Canadian government's attempts to discourage black people who wished to immigrate in the early nineteenth century. Nevertheless, she was a little surprised to hear at the 2017 reunion in Maidstone quiet rumours of a Klan revival. Some friends whispered to her, "We thought we'd better let you know." Such a revival had been chronicled by CBC Saskatchewan ten years earlier and more recently.[29]

The contemporary threat to a white-Protestant-only Saskatchewan that the KKK wishes to combat are Indigenous people or "Indians." They are increasingly the dominant faces, unwelcomed and targeted by some, in the urban centres of Regina, Saskatoon, Prince Albert, and North Battleford.

When Charlotte was growing up in North Battleford, black certainly was not the dominant face. However, while she remembers her family as being the only black family in the city, an exceptional family, she also recalls that colour didn't seem to be a factor in their lives. She wasn't really aware of her colour until she left North Battleford as a young adult.

Charlotte credits her own tenacity to the example of the family matriarch. One of the original settlers in 1910 was Mattie Mayes. She was the midwife for the entire area, for everybody, black and white and other. She was a force to be reckoned with and an important person not to offend. Charlotte remembers that Mattie lived to be 104 and was a "prayer warrior." Individuals were in her prayers, for comfort and consolation, as well as the discipline they needed. Mattie survived and gained respect in spite of hardships, prairie winters, and racism.[30]

Freed Slave Mattie Mayes (Provincial Archives of Saskatchewan R-A10361)

The Western College of Veterinary Medicine, part of the University of Saskatchewan and for all the western provinces, was postsecondary student Charlotte's destination: hoped for, prayed for, and studied for very hard. To be admitted into the college, one has to earn a high grade point average in the first two years of university, apply to the college, and then have an interview. Proclaims the catalogue:

As a regional veterinary college, the Western College of Veterinary Medicine accepts applicants who are residents of the four western provinces and the northern territories. Admission to the program is based on: Academic performance (minimum cumulative average of 75 per cent in all university courses), a structured interview designed to assess the applicant's abilities and strengths, insight into the profession, animal-related experience and knowledge and communication skills.[31]

Charlotte got one of the coveted spots. She credits her ability to walk through that exclusive door in part to her brother Reuben Mayes, a famous athletic and academic star from North Battleford, who went on to play in the NFL. He opened the door of the university for her. She didn't have to prove that a black person could excel. But Charlotte did have to keep excelling to stay there and graduate from the veterinary college.

The Mayes family has several more claims to fame. All seven children have done well. Charlotte says she is frequently described as "the first black woman veterinarian in Saskatchewan." Then she laughs. "But there was a South Asian woman in my class at U of Saskatchewan. She's black too." And when Charlotte was elected president of the Saskatchewan Veterinary Association, a friend observed that the world was certainly turning around! Obama was president of the United States, and Charlotte was a president too, the friend quipped. This observation surprised Charlotte because she hadn't been thinking about the powerful title; she had just intended to work for the good of her profession, her clients, and their animals.

Charlotte's husband, Earl, was a horticulturalist from the University of Saskatchewan, and the young Williams couple moved five times in five years for their work. They moved in Saskatoon, then to Biggar, then to Rosetown, and finally to Elrose. There was an incident in one of the small towns when Charlotte's sister was visiting and a passing car of teens yelled the "N" word. Charlotte, of course, had to seek out the perpetrators. She couldn't let that kind of thing go.[32]

The Williams family felt at home in Elrose. After a time, Charlotte opened a "small practice." It was hard at first. Elrose had never had a vet, certainly not a woman as a vet, and certainly not a black woman as a vet. Twenty-two years later she has the thriving business of Hooves and Paws.

Charlotte has had the major career. Earl has done "everything else," including looking after the three Williams children, the youngest now seventeen. Elrose, says Charlotte, has been a great place to bring up children. She thinks her children might have slipped through the cracks in an urban centre.

Charlotte would like to retire in ten years and is working on her succession plan. However, getting a new vet in rural Saskatchewan carries the same challenges as getting a new family physician. Her workload is heavy, and she's on call 24/7. Nevertheless, Charlotte is hopeful that a successor will be found or nurtured by her clinic.

Throughout my years in Saskatchewan, 1971–1989, I remained pretty much unaware of the black history of the

province. However, in 1985, through my union, the Alliance
of Canadian Cinema, TV, and Radio Artists (ACTRA), I
filed a discrimination grievance against the CBC. The issue
was that the producer of a docudrama about farm suicide
wouldn't let me audition because, he said, "there were no
black farmers in Saskatchewan." The case was finally settled out of court in my favour. And the National Farmers
Union (NFU) chapter based in the Maidstone vicinity
promised ACTRA that it would send a busload of people
to the planned arbitration to testify that there had been
and were black farmers in Saskatchewan. Perhaps the NFU's
promise is why the grievance was settled in our favour.

Charlotte says she would never consider moving to the
United States. When she visits there, it seems much more
chaotic, more like a police state, and you always have to
look out for yourself. Canada is much more inclusive, and
in rural Saskatchewan her children did not slip through
the cracks.

I asked Charlotte what the veterinary college was doing
about the blatant discrimination directed at Indigenous
people in education and all facets of Saskatchewan life.
She directed me to a recent provision of the college:
"The Aboriginal Equity Program encourages students of
Aboriginal descent to apply to the college. Spaces are available each year for Aboriginal students applying through
this program."[33]

So in 2017 there were rumours of a revival of the KKK
on the Prairies. The Mayes family has not been scared

away from Saskatchewan in 107 years. In fact, it has always stood up to discrimination. It seems unlikely that the family will be frightened now, especially Charlotte Mayes Williams of Elrose, whose investment in the inclusiveness of her community is wide, deep, and long.

INDIGENOUS LOYALTY:
DAN DAVID, KANEHSATÀ:KE

Simon Girty, patriarch of the Girty and Kennedy clans, whom we met earlier, impersonated a North American Indian for a good deal of his life. It was more serious than play-acting, as we found out from Pat Kennedy. Girty was adopted into the Seneca, one of the Six Nations, as are the Mohawk. Contemporary Mohawk Dan David, whose story we will hear in this section, cites Girty's adoption as speaking to his value and sincerity.

Then there is that famous impersonator Archie Belaney of Liverpool, known as Grey Owl. Belaney had no real Indigenous bloodline except through his wife.[34] Still, says Dan, Belaney became a celebrity, an early environmentalist and a naturalist who raised awareness through his books and speeches.

I don't have the training to psychoanalyze these men, nor is that the purpose of this book. However, here is a working theory of their almost obsessive need to identify with Indigenous people: the border and loyalties—who won, who lost, what they gained—and the legacy of colonialism can sometimes be too much for a person to hold together. Where Indigenous people are situated in the politics, philosophy, and social justice practices of North America is key to the story of American refugees. I paraphrase a curatorial note from a farsighted exhibition at the Simcoe County Historical Museum: We can debate who won the War of 1812 forever, one skirmish or another, several kilometres here or there. The Americans think they won. We are sure we did, especially Canadians from Simcoe County. Without a doubt, we know who lost. Indigenous people lost.

The history of betrayal of Indigenous people by Britain, the United States, and Canada, including along the world's longest undefended border, stretches from before settlement through the past and present colonial eras. Most of the American refugees profiled in this book have fled dangerous conditions in the United States, sided with the crown, greatly improved their lives in Canada, and then started to address unjust conditions here. For Indigenous people, however, the promises have usually been broken at every step. The Mohawk Nation is a classic example in central North America. Chief Sitting Bull is the classic example on the Prairies.

Sitting Bull and many of his people crossed the border into Canada after the battle at Little Big Horn, gathering at Wood Mountain. Sitting Bull was willing to be loyal to the Grandmother Queen as long as she was loyal to him and his people. He met (and became friends) with

North-West Mounted Police Inspector James Morrow
Walsh, who "assured him protection from the U.S. army
in exchange for peaceful compliance of Canadian law." But
when Sitting Bull requested a reserve for his people, the
Canadian government refused, "fearful that the chief's
presence would incite intertribal warfare and eager to clear
the Prairies for white settlement." The Canadian government broke faith with Sitting Bull not only by denying his
people a reserve, but also by denying food to the refugees gathered at Wood Mountain. Eventually, under threat
of starvation, Sitting Bull and his people returned to the
United States and settled on a reserve in North Dakota.[35]

The Mohawk sided with the crown through the War
of 1812 and beyond, but they, too, feel betrayed by the
Canadian government's reluctance to honour the 1794 Jay's
Treaty. Many Indigenous individuals, groups, and organizations have cited the treaty as a document that should
enable Indigenous people to travel without restrictions
across the contemporary Canada-US border. While "the
treaty is known for its provision that allows Aboriginal
people from Canada to live and work freely in the United
States…the Canadian federal government does not recognize the reciprocal provision as binding."[36]

Dan David is a member of a First Nation that values
and frequently seeks to preserve its relationship with and
loyalty to the crown; it also values its historical status as
a sovereign nation whose members can trade, work, and
visit without restrictions across the Canada-US border.

Dan's Mohawk ancestors expected their loyalty to the British to be remembered, a Canadian practice. They also expected Jay's Treaty to be respected, an American practice. Dan maintains those views in the face of all the challenges.

In the present era, I believe that where one places Indigenous issues in an understanding of the Canadian reality is the key philosophical, political, and human test. The tests of Indigenous loyalty to the crown go back a long way, to Sitting Bull, to the War of 1812, to Jay's Treaty. Canada frequently fails the test. It took a long time for me to understand the significance of this truth in Canadian history and experience. Indigenous realities are the frame around the experiences of all the American refugees. Dan David has been a great help in my understanding of those realities. However, as a black person from the American South, when I travelled from northern Ontario to the prairies in the 1970s, I quickly identified with racism directed at Indigenous peoples, and this identification led to years of chronicling Indigenous issues in my media career.

I detailed my deepening education about the Canadian denial of racism in my essay entitled "Slavery Endangers the Master's Health, but Please Don't Shoot the Messenger," published by the Aboriginal Healing Foundation in 2011 in *Cultivating Canada: Reconciliation through the Lens of Cultural Diversity*. For me, the main truth revealed was the chronic Canadian blind spot about Canada and its ongoing treatment of Indigenous peoples. This excerpt from that essay recalls my first encounters with this blind spot upon my arrival in Thunder Bay:

1971–72

There are shadowy brown people creeping around the edge of what feels like a USA Wild West town square. In my mind's eye, it resembles 1940s Texas, where I grew up.

But focus. Get a grip, woman. This is not Texas. This is Canada, my new country, the 1970s. This is Thunder Bay, Ontario. I am still black; however, these brown people are not Afro-Canadians.

Regina is my final destination this first trip west from Toronto, and there I come to understand that these mysterious brown people are Aboriginal. The déjà vu feeling is correct though. Aboriginal persons are literally and figuratively on the margins. They are excluded from the centre of society's hustle and bustle.

In those days I was an actress and thrilled beyond words to have been hired by Regina's professional theatre, The Globe. It was not easy for black and other visible minority actors working in *mainstream* theatre back then, and not much easier now....

1971: only three years have passed since the assassination of Martin Luther King Jr., and memories of the civil rights era are still fresh. Many Regina citizens still have vivid memories of news footage featuring police dogs, fire hoses, and angry mobs shaking their fists at little black girls. When Saskatchewanites mentally connect me with this racial trauma they've witnessed on television, they begin to chant with passion and compassion, "We are not racist" (in Canada). Quickly I discover that these same *not racist* people believe that Indians are all on welfare, are lazy and shiftless, are not pro-active about their children's educations, have messy family lives, and are drunks. I tell at least three individuals per day that these attitudes directed at an identifiable group constitute racism. They have become convinced that only if their negative feelings are directed at black people, of whom there are almost none in Regina, are they being racist. "Racism" and "Aboriginal people" are not yet terms that can be logically linked together for most folk.[37]

A CANADIAN CITIZENSHIP CEREMONY, 2018

Now I am faced with trying to impart to new citizens, before I swear them in, some of the lessons from my years of chronicling Indigenous issues. Certainly, naturalized citizens of my era, the 1960s and 1970s, were not faced with the elephants in the spacious Canadian rooms: stolen land, colonization, residential schools, cultural genocide, obviously more than two founding peoples. Ironically, because of the 2015 Truth and Reconciliation Commission reports and recent changes in the materials studied to become a Canadian citizen, the newest immigrants may learn more of the truth than those in any previous era. Standing in the Royal Ontario Museum, an institution that has taken the lead in repatriating Indigenous sacred materials, this is what I say to the assembly of candidates for citizenship on July 1, Canada Day, 2018:

> One of our responsibilities is to pay back: to recognize that we are here because Aboriginal peoples, Inuit, Métis, and First Nations, welcomed us and continue to share their territories. Another of our responsibilities is to pay forward by becoming as involved as we can in the many communities that are Canada.
>
> *Our history, frequently glorious and sometimes unfortunate*, is now your history. Our laws are your laws. Our identity is your identity. Our responsibility to be a good, faithful, and active citizen, loyal to Canada, is now your responsibility.

MY STORY CONTINUES:
MEETING DAN DAVID IN REGINA

Dan David is a writer, journalist, media trainer, producer, a citizen of the Six Nations Confederacy, and, as we will learn, a citizen of the world. I first met Dan when he was posted to CBC Regina from 1983 to 1986, his first job after being in CBC's "Visible Minority Training Program." Someone suggested he contact me about the racist goings-on in the Queen City's newsroom. In those days,

Dan would come back from lunch and find handwritten notes (from his CBC colleagues) in his typewriter carriage that said, "Go back where you came from!" I don't know how much wisdom I was able to provide beyond some deep laughter about the situation, refreshing libations in my living room, and the suggestion of a wise and credible executive at CBC who would put a stop to such stupid racist behaviour. In any case, Dan and I remained friends and, at times, colleagues, including when he encouraged me in 2002 to sit in a chair he had recently vacated: director of news and current affairs at APTN, with a mandate to mentor my Indigenous successor and kick-start the daily *APTN National News.*

My most recent conversation with Dan was during the floods in Quebec in May 2017. He was part of an all-out community effort—bailing, sandbagging—to keep his community of Kanehsatà:ke safe and dry. Dan and his brother had spent a good deal of the past year making speeches on impending environmental crises. They let settler groups in Quebec and Ontario know that floods were on the way, that how we have treated waterways and built dams will catch up with us.

Kanehsatà:ke succeeded in keeping itself dry in 2017, for the most part because of the massive community effort in which Dan was involved. The community did not take up the offer of the Canadian army to help them as it helped the neighbouring town of Oka. Said Dan: "I didn't have a problem with military help during this spring's floods.

I know that people who had homes flooded didn't have a problem either. Most people on the territory understood and distinguished the difference between flood aid and military-backed government oppression."[38] However, the elected leaders rejected help from the military.

An exhausted Dan said he can't spend so much time on environmental activism anymore. Not many people are listening anyway, he commented. But maybe the floods have changed that. In this volunteer work, Dan was being loyal to his territory and his ancestors. The world's longest undefended border is not his concept. Ancestors and territory frame his worldview.

Dan David (Courtesy of Dan David)

Dan David and his people actively dispute whether the Canada-us border is a border at all for them. At the same time, they take part of their identity from a "Loyalist" past, from what the crown (Canada) owes them for that loyalty. Both of these historical matters of identity go largely unrecognized by others. Since the Indigenous story is counter to the border stories that we as Canadians like to tell ourselves, only infrequently do we tell or even acknowledge it. In this story, who won or lost the War of 1812 is not important, but the loyalties are. To the present day, that relationship with the crown is tested. The Mohawk sided with the crown and against those revolutionaries in the United States who were forcing them north and west. The settler Loyalists (white people) were rewarded for their loyalty; black Loyalists, as we've seen, were sometimes partially rewarded; Indigenous peoples were not and are not rewarded. Canada, particularly under the government of Stephen Harper from 2005 to 2015, liked to say we have no colonial history and thus no colonization story.

From Dan's perspective, neither country has respected Indigenous peoples, and both have created long-lasting, multi-tiered citizenship processes. The community of Akwesasne near Cornwall, Ontario, is unlike any other in North America because it straddles seven distinct jurisdictions: the United States and Canada; the State of New York; the Provinces of Ontario and Quebec; the St. Regis Mohawk Tribal Council; and the Akwesasne

Mohawk Council. Despite these foreign-made divisions, there are Mohawk clans, families, and individuals who try hard to remember they are one people and one community. The sovereignty of the territory has been part of Haudenosaunee Confederacy memory since time immemorial, but specifically since the 1920s, when the Six Nations applied to the League of Nations. That application didn't succeed, but the beliefs behind it have not changed.

A Mohawk Man on an Overturned Police Vehicle, 1990
(Canadian Press/Paul Chiasson)

Before the Oka stand-off of 1990, Dan recalls, the times were simpler, gentler. But that summer, everything changed for him. The proposed expansion of the Oka golf course was threatening a Mohawk cemetery and a

100-year-old pine forest on Mohawk territory. The people of Kanehsatà:ke responded with a protest, then occupation of the disputed land. The situation escalated to a confrontation with police and the armed forces. Dan and some of his family members were among those behind the barricades.

Twenty-five years later, Dan recalled those days in a piece he wrote for CBC *News*:

> At 5 a.m. on the morning of July 11, I'll be with traditional people and a few guests in The Pines on Kanehsatà:ke Mohawk Territory. There won't be any government people, politicians, or members of the band council.
>
> No long speeches, preening egos, or empty promises allowed. Just a few people who wish to reflect on the meanings of events that began on a day exactly 25 years before.
>
> Each person will offer tobacco to a fire, share thoughts with the Creator. After everyone has done so, they'll put the fire out and leave.
>
> That's the way it's been and will be this year, next year, and the one after that until the next confrontation provides new reasons to remember.
>
> On July 11, 1990, my world became a lot more black and white as a writer and journalist. The actions of Canada and Quebec shattered most of the illusions I'd been taught about a "Just Society," the "rule of law," and "honour of the Crown."[39]

Whatever else can be said of the Oka stand-off, it remains iconic of how Canada/Quebec views Kanehsatà:ke Mohawk territory.

For Dan, his relationship with the border similarly changed after he was awarded a Commonwealth Fellowship. He emerged from the life-changing events at Oka to learn that he was a recipient of the prestigious honour. Dan needed travel documents to go to London to accept the prize, which included trips to several South Pacific nations of the Commonwealth, and to be presented to Queen Elizabeth II in Buckingham Palace. Conflicting loyalties and broken promises were again part of the story, as Dan explained to me in an email:

> …the main reason for my not taking a Canadian passport was the Canadian Government's insistence that I renounce my Mohawk citizenship in order to do so. As an adult, I could have done so without much fuss. But Canada insisted I get my parents to sign sworn affidavits that they were "Canadian" as well. There was a choice to be made. In the end, another senior official in the Canadian Government told me to just get the American passport, accept the Fellowship, go to London, and "don't worry because all will be worked out." Once there, however, Canada changed its mind again. I faxed a letter that night, the night before we were scheduled to go to Buckingham Palace, telling Canadian officials that I would rip up my American passport, go to *The Times* of London and play

them a tape of these senior Canadian government officials telling me to take the US Passport, etc. I would declare myself stateless, a political refugee from Canada, and raise all kinds of hell internationally across Europe.[40]

As Dan faced this difficult situation, he did so with a profound sense of his own family history: in 1902 his great-grandfather, Kanawatiron, had also travelled to Buckingham Palace, a fugitive from Canadian authorities. He carried with him a petition which he wanted to deliver in person to King Edward VII, on behalf of all the chiefs of the Longhouse of Kanehsatà:ke, asking that the King and the government of Canada would honour their promises and commitments to his nation. Dan has told this story in his moving essay "All My Relations," where he recounts:

[Kanawatiron] shows up unannounced at the gates of Buckingham Palace. He holds a petition in his hand. He wears his best English-cut, double-breasted suit with a handkerchief folded neatly into his breast pocket. A guard arrives to ask his business. Kanawatiron hands him a letter of introduction with his signature, Joseph K. Gabriel, in a long, flowing hand above the X's and names of the other chiefs of the Longhouse of Kanehsatà:ke.

But the king sends word he will not see my great-grandfather. The royal guard tells him he is not a British subject. He instructs my great-grandfather to go to the American embassy instead.

"What good can the king do?" inquires a reporter.

"Is he not the king?" asks Kanawatiron. "...He can do everything."[41]

Dan's great-grandfather never did receive his audience with the king, and he returned to Canada, where he continued to fight the authorities, harassed by police and government officials "until the end."[42] Kanawatiron was buried under the pine trees in the very cemetery that his descendants occupied when it was threatened with bulldozing to make way for an expanded golf course in 1990.

When Dan found himself in London, also at risk of being refused an audience with the reigning monarch, he took courage from his memories of his great-grandfather's story. The story continues in "All My Relations":

That night, I type a letter. I do the same thing my great-grandfather would have done....I fax the letter to Canada House.

The next day, an official calls on me and says that my situation is causing some problems and embarrassment in Ottawa. "Good," I say...."After 1990, you don't think I'd really trust anybody from the Canadian government, do you?"...

Whatever happens, I am my great-grandfather's granddaughter's son. I'm walking in his footsteps. I know he wants—finally—to be welcomed into Buckingham Palace.

In the morning: "I've got good news," an official of the Commonwealth tells me. "You can complete your fellowship. You'll accompany us to our audience with the queen tomorrow."…

The doors swing open. I stroll down the length of this huge room toward a little, grey-haired woman in a summer dress. She looks surprisingly like my mother. I stop and nod.

"Are you some kind of an Indian?" she asks in that familiar voice.

"Yes, I am, Your Majesty," I reply, slightly confused, but pulling myself up to my full height. "I'm from Canada."

"Oh," she continues. "What kind of an Indian are you?"

"A Mohawk," I say.

"A Mohawk." She pauses slightly. "You're not one of those naughty Mohawks, are you?"

I wait for a second before answering "Yes, ma'am, I am."[43]

It took four generations, but for an instant Dan David was able to negotiate the appropriate relationship between his people and the crown and his people and the Canada-US border.[44] A Mohawk citizen who frequently lives on his home territory, Dan has been speaking truth to power his entire career as a journalist in Canada and continues to do so:

If we're a "difficult people" it may be because we have
a strong sense of identity and know our own history.
Canada's (and the United States') attempts to erase us
from their history books…and create a fictional "Indian"
in literature, art, film and other media succeeded but
only with their own populations. We've been consistently "difficult" as a result. We take pride in that fact.[45]

Dan has pointed out that, regardless of the constant
reminders, especially by Canada, that "my identity is
unrecognized and worthless, we serve, fight for, and die
for both countries in surprising numbers despite these
histories."[46]

The Mohawk people did not get what they were promised in either the Revolutionary War or the War of 1812.
However, as an individual, Dan accomplished much in
his career and received a Commonwealth Fellowship. The
immense challenges of loyalties play out on a daily basis:
remaining loyal to the crown that negotiated Jay's Treaty,
which allows free cross-border access; remaining loyal to
settlers in Canada who occupy and still need to learn how
to care for the land of the promises. The border? *What border?* Dan could talk about the subject forever.

Canada has always had great difficulty maintaining its
"best country" image when Indigenous people shatter the
supposedly perfect picture. Yet, any analysis of the world's
longest undefended border must include them. American
refugees, settlers in Canada, discover what has to be put

right. Which promises are made and then kept or broken, which allies are desirable, and whether Canada's social safety net is inclusive—all of these must be considered.

Dan's territory, though? The loyalties there are clear. And they include loyalty to those settler guests in Ontario and Quebec and New York who have been warned about environmental disaster by the First Nation that straddles their borders.

AMERICAN
LOYALTY TESTED
THE MCCARTHY ERA

███

MY STORY CONTINUES:
SO MUCH TO OVERCOME BY SO FEW

At least two biographical themes draw the refugees and immigrants in this section together. First, the catalyst for their move to Canada was the McCarthy era: the federal House Committee on Un-American Activities and the state committees, the Cold War, the socialist/communist witch hunts of the 1940s and 1950s. Second, they were all involved in the black Civil Rights movement of the same era, continuing into the 1960s.

Although my own story has been dominated at times by civil rights struggles and continual racial problems in the United States and Canada, my connection to the McCarthy era did not become conscious until I moved to Saskatchewan. There, in 1971, I met Florence Bean James, a theatre person who had been deeply involved with equality rights for black people, including with Paul Robeson, and who had been driven out of the United States by the Washington State Committee on Un-American Activities. One can come to the conclusion that what was un-American about the victims of McCarthyism was their advocacy of equal rights, especially for black people, plus women and other non-dominant groups.

I'll begin this chapter by sharing three excerpts from my first one-woman play, *Smoked Glass Ceiling*, which chronicles how a little black girl was taught to survive the racist American South. The first excerpt recalls a moment from my childhood; the second relives racial discrimination in my teen years in Houston, with the focus on what's most important to me, the arts; the third recounts parallel discrimination when I was in late middle age in Canada. The other stories that follow in this chapter—on the Lorch-Bartels family, Florence Bean James, and Sara Diamond—all echo my story. Each is characterized by an early American problem (reason to flee) and their later discovery of a problem in Canada (cause for activism).

Smoked Glass Ceiling, SCENE #2, June 19, 1951

On the 19th of June each year I ask how far have I come
from slavery? How far?

For a long time after I left Houston in 1962 my father
would ask anxiously on the Juneteenth: "Baby do you
know what day it is?"

He thought, I guess, that things had changed so much in
his lifetime—Daddy was 93 when he died—that I could
not be old enough to remember what it was like before
the civil rights movement.

But I remembered.

The 19th of June 1951. I am 6 years old.

This is the one day of the year that Black Texan children were allowed in to an amusement park named
Playland. The kind of place I wouldn't be caught dead in
once I had the freedom to go. Tacky, loud, dirty, speed,
and games of chance that reek of false risk and pretend
competition.

The one day Black Texans could go to the movie theatres and sit in on the first floor, not in the balcony.
The state was closed on this one day to white people,

Emancipation Day, and open to Black people. We had freedom for a day.

Our family did not take advantage of this one day windfall. What we had was better. Big celebrations of family and friends. Movies shown on our own 16 mm projector to the people, the children, we invited.

My mother's lifelong philosophy was "what I am denied I will build myself." For me, my family, and as many friends as Mother could gather up. So we had a pre–civil rights "home entertainment centre," sponsored by segregation.[1]

SCENE #3, June 19, 1961 (Houston)

The South being allegedly open for business by 1960 I presented myself to the registrar at the Alley Theatre Academy—naturally for the purpose of studying acting.

Apart from giving the somewhat elderly lady registrar there cardiac arrest, though it took a few months to work this out, I found a whole nest of mentors. She called help! Help! Help! to the Associate Artistic Director. There's a little black girl standing in the lobby trying to register for an acting class. Whatever shall I do in this crisis?

Faced with the necessity of clearing me out of the lobby the director said why don't you volunteer at the theatre itself? "Forget the classes." And that was where I spent every evening and weekend for the next 2 years....

There was an awful lot of work to do at that theatre. Lights and sound to learn how to run. Props to make. A new floor to paint with every new play. Warm-ups to learn. Equity apprenticeship classes to get into. And, finally, coaching for a scholarship to university.

I had a whole company of mature first-rate actors—I now know guilt-ridden about the crime of racial segregation in their country—to prepare me.[2]

SCENE #8, 2000 (Toronto)

The Queen Bee is in action, building a productive hive— that's what Vice Presidents of Production DO—for a bunch of multi-racial workers and drones. And that is enough for me for 12 years. Productivity, creativity, hard work is still the mantra.

I've spent almost a half a century living out my destiny as a Queen Bee, until I'm very close to the top of the corporate heap. Now the top job is open: the Head Honcho, the Big Kahoonah, the Chief Poobah, The Man....

What I experience is a variation on the immigrant job run-around that is so rare as to be in a class by itself.

The executive head hunting firm says: "You don't get the job because you have no previous CEO experience. We're only going to make an offer to someone with previous CEO experience."

The executive head hunters hyperventilate: Help. There's a little black girl here in the executive lobby—with the Persian carpet, mahogany furniture, brass pots, and chilled designer water—and she wants to be a CEO. Help! Help! Help! There's a little black girl. Help.

There's a girl. Help....[3]

The little black girl from the American South uses the same techniques, learned from her mother, to survive in cool grey Canadian boardrooms. The techniques work, up to a point. I have to admit, as the writer-performer of *Smoked Glass Ceiling*, with thirty-five performances between 2005 and 2010, I am always surprised at how funny it is to audiences and to me while it is being performed.

There is nothing funny, of course, about my experiences of racism, sexism, and power plays. And there is nothing funny about the experiences of those whom we'll meet in the next sections: the cross burnings on the Lorch lawn, the conviction of Florence Bean James for contempt of an un-American committee, and the doors to better employment shut tight for the parents of Sara Diamond. But all of these survivors have remarkable resilience. We'll hear about these serious issues, then the newcomers' wonderful welcome to Canada, and then their later discovery of different, much more polite, challenges of social justice here.

THE LORCHES AND BARTELS:
TWO GENERATIONS OF REFUGEES

The small family of three never wanted to leave the United States. But they had to, finally. No jobs for father. He'd been eased out of at least five American universities, two of them all-black schools. Dr. Lee Lorch, a gifted mathematician, and Mrs. Grace Lorch, a passionate public school teacher, had supported racial integration all of their adult lives, putting conviction into action. Walking the talk. Those convictions turned out to be both physically dangerous and grounds for firing, loss of income. And those convictions eventually drove the family out of the US and turned them north to Canada.

In 1957, one particular incident threw the Lorches, especially Grace, into the hot lights of news cameras. As members of the Little Rock, Arkansas, NAACP, Lee and Grace Lorch were helping to enroll nine high school students (known later as the "Little Rock Nine") who attempted to be the first black students at Little Rock Central High School. Grace stood up to the angry white mobs who had gathered to protest and was seen in a famous photograph that went around the world. *New York Times* journalist

Benjamin Fine was there to cover the story. This is his account of the events, as it appears in the memoir of Daisy Bates, who at the time was president of the Arkansas branch of the NAACP:

> Suddenly I saw a white-haired, kind-faced woman fighting her way through the mob. She looked at Elizabeth, and then screamed at the mob, "Leave this child alone! Why are you tormenting her? Six months from now, you will hang your heads in shame." The mob shouted, "Another nigger-lover. Get out of here!" The woman, who I found out later was Mrs. Grace Lorch, the wife of Dr. Lee Lorch, professor at Philander Smith College, turned to me and said, "We have to do something. Let's try to get a cab."
>
> We took Elizabeth across the street to the drugstore. I remained on the sidewalk with Elizabeth while Mrs. Lorch tried to enter the drugstore to call a cab. But the hoodlums slammed the door in her face and wouldn't let her in. She pleaded with them to call a cab for the child. They closed in on her saying, "Get out of here, you bitch!" Just then the city bus came. Mrs. Lorch and Elizabeth got on. Elizabeth must have been in a state of shock. She never uttered a word.[4]

In response to her actions, Grace received letters of praise from across North America and as far away as New Zealand and Belgium. Many well-wishers followed the extensive media coverage of the events in Little Rock in 1957. Those letters are now in the York University archives.[5]

Grace Lorch Protecting Little Rock High School Student Elizabeth Eckford, 1957 (Permission from the University of Arkansas at Little Rock, Center for Arkansas History and Culture)

The Little Rock incident made Grace very visible, but she had a history of taking activist stances. Shortly after her marriage to Lee, she appealed a school board ruling that "full-time female teachers could not be married," a policy that forced her out of her chosen profession.

"Although her appeal was not successful, it set the stage for challenges by other Boston teachers and, eventually, reversal of the rule by the Massachusetts legislature."[6]

Alice Lorch (far right) at Fisk University Experimental School, 1952–53 (Lorch-Bartels family photo)

And together, Lee and Grace took a number of principled positions that had real consequences for them and for their young daughter, Alice. They were a unit. Alice was part of her parents' activist lifestyle from childhood. Lee and Grace believed in integrated housing and sublet their apartment in New York City's Stuyvesant Town to a black family. Lee lost his job at City College. They believed in integrated schools. Their preteen daughter, Alice, went to a black school. And Lee Lorch worked for equality for black scholars and for women in his field of mathematics.

Then, as McCarthyism took hold in the US, the family was charged with un-American activities. Alice certainly had a unique childhood, similar to the world of the black children who integrated Little Rock High School. She was an "only" and a "first" to cross a number of lines. In 2015 Alice was interviewed by *NOW* magazine about her family's experiences at this time:

> Alice Bartels was 13 when she accompanied her mother, Grace Lorch, from their home in Little Rock, Arkansas, to Memphis, Tennessee. The teacher and civil rights activist had been subpoenaed to appear before a southern sitting of the U.S. Senate's Internal Security Subcommittee.
>
> "It was just like that Arthur Miller play [*The Crucible*]," Bartels recalls of the subcommittee hearing. "A bunch of white men sitting up on high, treating everyone else down below with contempt."
>
> A series of witnesses were mistreated by the subcommittee, including an elderly man who was cited for contempt because he did not answer questions he could not hear. Bartels says her mother, who was there under protest, told the subcommittee she had a statement to read, but members of the committee would start yelling

at her. "They threatened to indict her for contempt of
the Senate, and that was held over her head for a year."…

Bartels says she was "worried my mother would get
sent to jail, which was a nightmare to me. Somehow my
father's going to jail seemed more normal, though I was
pretty worried about him, too." Such fears were a constant, as her parents' refusal to abide by segregation cost
them jobs, made them the target of hateful threats and
forced frequent moves to find work.[7]

Alice recalls, too, that many of the white people of
Little Rock were actually very kind and put their lives on
the line for the Lorches. When crosses were burned on the
Lorch family's lawn, neighbours found the family members other places to live.

Eventually, Dr. Lorch elected to leave his final job in the
United States at a black college because he didn't want to
put the president in any further danger. After dealing with
McCarthyism and Civil Rights backlash over segregated
housing and education, the family decided to leave the
country. The reality is, there were no jobs for them. The
Department of Mathematics at the University of Alberta
welcomed them. So did a couple of other Canadian universities, but U of A made the most financially rewarding
offer to this family who had been in very unstable economic situations for several years.

I am struck by two realities in the biographies of the
Lorches. First, they never took time out from their fights

against injustice. This would have been possible since they were white and in physical danger. But it seems that this was precisely why Lee and Grace could not stop, could not give up. Since they were equally committed to struggles for social justice, they chose not to give up. They didn't ever give up.

Second, I am surprised that all of Lee's battles to support women and people of colour in professional associations and universities were in mathematics. As a naive artist, I always assumed, held a prejudice, in fact, that the hard sciences were more rational. The scientists, I thought, were less discriminatory. They would accept anyone with the right talent. Who could or would argue with the numbers? Wrong. Lee had to work for years to get visible minorities and women recognized in professional math associations. He was finally applauded and received awards for his advocacy on behalf of non-discrimination, including an award for Distinguished Service to Mathematics in 2007. The citation for that award reads, in part:

> Throughout his career [Dr. Lorch] has been a vocal advocate and energetic worker for human rights and educational opportunities. His interventions, especially in the 1950's, led to changes in…policies and practices.…
>
> As an example, we cite events surrounding a meeting in 1951 held in Nashville. Lee Lorch, the chair of the mathematics department at Fisk University, and three Black colleagues…came to the meeting and were able to

attend the scientific sessions. However, the organizer for
the closing banquet refused to honor the reservations of
these four mathematicians....Lorch and his colleagues
wrote to the governing bodies of the AMS and MAA
seeking bylaws against discrimination. Bylaws were not
changed, but non-discriminatory policies were established and have been strictly observed since then.[8]

Lee Lorch was tireless in seeking equality rights for
women and people of colour in his professional mathematics associations. Unlike segregated housing and public schools, these were the power structures closest to
him, and he went to great lengths to get them to change
their practices.

The family, finely attuned to racism after their years
in the United States, also found it in their new country, Canada, in 1958, where it was primarily levelled
at Indigenous peoples. The family's interests began to
include Indigenous matters. Lee helped to found the
Edmonton Native Friendship Centre shortly after moving
to Alberta. After his move to Toronto and York University
all of the social justice initiatives continued. Much later,
in Newfoundland, Alice and her husband, Dennis Bartels,
researched part of the history that would assist the Qalipu
Mi'kmaq First Nation to stake its claims. They later wrote
a book entitled *When the North Was Red: Aboriginal
Education in Soviet Siberia*. In short, the family never gave
up, never tired of its activism against discrimination.

Dennis Bartels, now a senior in Toronto, was a Vietnam War resister who immigrated to Alberta in 1963. He says he went from near starvation in the United States to a living wage in Alberta. Dennis and Alice have asked their adult children if they could see themselves moving to the United States. Their answer is that they never think of moving there. After their arrival in Alberta, Lee and Grace and later Dennis and Alice were extremely fortunate in the individuals whom they met and the institutions that embraced them. The University of Alberta hired the gifted mathematician Lee. Daughter Alice and mother Grace felt welcomed in social activist leadership roles.

When he was in his nineties, Lee was asked in a videotaped interview what advice he had for activists. His answer? "Don't give up. Never give up. It ain't over till it's over. And many decent folk come out of the woodwork. It's easy to remember the phonies. But there are more decent folk."[9] The Lorches always seemed to look for and find decent folk to take an anti-discrimination stance. They were eternally optimistic about the number of such people in the world. Perhaps that is what kept them going for so long.

The Lorches and Bartels have all been activists. That's how and why they got to Canada. They were eager to embrace the freedom and openness of Canadian society. Yet they also found limits to that openness almost immediately, especially concerning Indigenous people throughout Canadian history and, more recently, towards Iraq

War resisters. Canadians, for the most part, welcomed the more than 50,000 Americans, including Dennis Bartels, who refused to serve in the Vietnam War from 1965 to 1973, but the Canadian government had a much different response to those Americans who did not want to serve in the Iraq War and thus sought asylum in Canada from 2003 to 2011.[10] Dennis, along with other Vietnam resisters whom we will meet in the next chapter, has been vocal about Canada's hostile treatment of Iraq resisters. Predictably, the Lorches and Bartels took up the Indigenous and Iraq cases of discrimination in Canadian society with their life-long activist dedication.

FLORENCE BEAN JAMES:
ALMOST TALKED MYSELF INTO JAIL

I have researched and written about Florence Bean James, born in Pocatello, Idaho, in 1892, for the past forty-five years. Moreover, she has been my arts and life mentor, muse, and role model from the moment I recorded her history until the present.

"Mrs. James," as she was usually called, entered my consciousness in 1971 when I was in rehearsal in Regina for the Globe Theatre School Tour. She was then a very elderly lady snoozing at the back of the Centre of the Arts rehearsal room. Initially what glued me to her, once I had this information, was that she and her husband had founded and run The Negro Repertory, funded by the

Works Progress Administration in Seattle in the 1930s. As a theatre person who is black, I knew how absolutely revolutionary this was.

Florence Bean James lived a truly remarkable life during a seemingly irrational era that is still being analyzed. As a young woman, she left her rural home to study elocution at Emerson College in Boston, where she met her future husband, Burton James, an aspiring actor. Together, they developed their vision of a community theatre. As Florence says in the opening chapter of her memoir, "Burton and I had been working all our adult lives, first in New York, then in Seattle, toward a theatre that would be of the people, by the people, and for the people."[11] This dream was at last realized in 1928 when they launched their Seattle Repertory Playhouse. For twenty years, they brought world-class theatre to Washington State, emphasizing education, egalitarianism, and community involvement. The "Red Scare" of the late 1940s and 1950s destroyed their lifelong creative work, as they were called before the Canwell Committee (the Washington State Committee on Un-American Activities). Their theatre was bankrupt, their livelihood gone, and Burton's health quickly failed. He died in late 1951. In 1952, Florence came to Canada, to Saskatchewan, a refugee from McCarthyism, who at the age of sixty miraculously had over thirty more years of energy, drive, and inspiration to offer to her adopted country.

My fascination with Florence resulted in thirty half hours of reel-to-reel taped interviews with her and those

who knew her in the 1970s and 1980s; writing and performing a one-woman, one-act play entitled *McCarthy
and the Old Woman* (2008); writing a full-length play of
the same title (2010); and producing a *Bravo!fact* nationally broadcast drama short (2007).[12] What follow here
are excerpts from my full-length play; from a not-yet-
produced screenplay about Florence; and from the epilogue that I wrote for Florence's memoir, *Fists Upon a Star:
A Memoir of Love, Theatre, and Escape from McCarthyism,*
which was co-authored with Jean Freeman and published
in 2013 by the University of Regina Press. That publication
happened after a long and complicated history. Jean had
been taught drama as a teen by Florence, resulting in lifelong respect, friendship, and support for the elderly Mrs.
James. We tried from the 1980s to get *Fists Upon a Star*
published. Nobody would touch it. Looking back on our
publishing odyssey, I think American publishers weren't
ready to examine the McCarthy era. And Canadian publishers didn't see why a theatre story from the Prairies was
important. The climate changed in the 2000s, perhaps
with feature films such as *Goodnight and Good Luck* and
Trumbo. And URP publisher Bruce Walsh instantly saw
why Florence's memoir was significant.

    In fact, the focus of this entire book is captured in a
statement made about Florence in a lengthy obituary written by distinguished arts journalist Mavor Moore in the
Globe and Mail: "We've paid very little attention to the
phenomenon [Florence James] personified: the benign

American invasion of Canada that accompanied the McCarthy years in the United States."[13] The fallout from McCarthyism does seem to crystallize problems in the United States that have been reinforced and reinvented until the present day: racism; opposition to the socialist philosophy of caring for all citizens, including health care, education, and cultural life; and waging war. Florence dealt with all of these problems in her art and her politics. She also found a final career and resting place in Saskatchewan, where her worldview and skills were totally needed and welcomed. Enter Rita and Florence in the theatre, not the political arena.

MY STORY CONTINUES: MEETING FLORENCE BEAN JAMES AT THE GLOBE

Two excerpts follow from my play about Florence, *McCarthy and the Old Woman*, produced in 2010 in the same theatre building in Seattle that Florence and Burton James built and from which they were brutally removed and blacklisted. First, the Rita character, in her twenties, reveals her reactions to this "old white woman" when she meets her in 1971 in the Globe Theatre rehearsal hall.

FLORENCE
Speak up please?!
What *are* you saying for pity sakes?
I'm way back here 6 rows. It's not that far.

RITA
(to audience)
Who is this Old Lady telling us to speak up? Us,
newly minted professional actors.

I've got my first card-carrying Equity job! It feels
like I've died and gone to heaven.

OK. I'm more than a little nervous—terrified
actually—about doing a classical play—me
from Texas!—with folk straight from Canada's
National Theatre School.

But, I'm pumped to prove and double prove
to the Globe Theatre and Canadian theatre in
general that it cannot do without me.

FLORENCE
Speak up!

RITA
You've likely noticed that I'm Black. By 1971,
lusting for the professional theatre since I was
16, I don't think this miracle will ever happen to
me. The miracle is more than worth the move
from Toronto to Regina.

Everything seems to be going OK in the first of
four weeks. In the second week the Director
tells us that the little old lady sitting in the back
of the rehearsal hall can't hear us. We should
"speak up."

                    FLORENCE
          (really irascible)
Speak Up.

                    RITA
I haven't a clue who she is. And nobody is
bothering to tell our happy little band of five
actors. Somebody's mother maybe? The theatre
using rehearsals as a seniors' day care for
somebody's mother?

                    FLORENCE
Speak Up!

                    RITA
My fellow actors just aren't worried?

                    RITA
          (to audience)
But, I have to know how much power this
old woman has over me. Is this very white,

white-haired old lady—probably racist and
bigoted to the back of her likely false teeth—
going to get me fired? Fired from the miracle
Equity job.

Seems to me the other confident—white—actors
just preen, pretend, and listen for the helicopter
wings that will magic them from the wilds of
Saskatchewan to dead centre on the Stratford
Festival stage.

Anyway, I finally have to ask the Director:
The silver-haired lady, with the er...helpful...
notes...who is she?

Scene 5, the Rehearsal Hall, Globe Theatre

RITA
(to audience)

I cannot make head nor tail of this. It's such
a dog's breakfast of names and accusations.
Everything from staging ordinary proscenium
plays to rumours of terrorism. Maybe Mrs.
James' memory is faulty. Throughout that entire
summer when I tape her, I wanted to know what
she *did*. It seemed bizarre. People were charged
and jailed for doing the very theatre work I
wanted so desperately to do.

I don't know a lot about the blacklist. My
Mother is embarrassed and surprised to find out
that I thought the Black-List happened only to
White-People. She asks me (*mother's voice*) "if,
perhaps, I'd heard of Brother Paul Robeson?"[14]

My mother, Versie Powell Shelton, when she visited
Regina from Houston, was quite disgusted that it took my
meeting Florence to become aware of the McCarthy era.
She thought that I knew more, especially about those warriors who did so much for civil rights.

RITA'S MOTHER
Child, you *do* know that there were black people
right here in Houston who were blacklisted?
Most of them were Democrats. Most of them
moved about the town just as they pleased—
ignoring segregation.

You remember Mrs. Adair don't you, very
high up in the Democratic Party. And the
Covingtons, Dr. and Mrs. Covington, who
hosted Marion Anderson when she couldn't sing
in any auditorium or stay in any hotel.

RITA
Er…not quite…

RITA'S MOTHER

Well you should remember. Good grief, I took
you over to the house so you could meet Miss
Anderson. Did I waste my time?

RITA
(to audience)

Cut me some slack please! Of course I
remember meeting the great contralto—I was
four years old, and I've seen pictures. But I *don't*
remember the blacklist.

My memories and understanding of the
McCarthy era are fuzzy. As a young child in the
'50s in the United States, it is actually weird.
My elementary school in Houston drills us in
climbing under our desks in case the "godless
Communist Russians" should make our 5th
ward ghetto a bomb target. Anything was
possible with those crazies.

I am way too young to analyze an entire era that still
baffles thousands of bright grown-ups. The era later
called the cold war, and depending who you were
talking to, remembered for naming names, loyalty
oaths, blacklists, witch-hunts and "McCarthyism"—for Senator Joseph McCarthy, Chair of the
national Un-American Activities Committee.[15]

███

Every seat was taken at Florence's memorial service in Regina in 1988. However, that well-attended event did not unite her many worlds, her politics, and her arts practice. But her life in Saskatchewan did. In my epilogue to *Fists Upon a Star*, I tried to analyze the force of nature that was the arrival of Florence in Saskatchewan, her perfect home (the italicized text below represents Florence's own words, from the taped interviews):

Seven decades have passed since Florence Bean James arrived in Regina and her newly adopted Canada to work and live until her last breath. "Mrs. James," as she was most frequently addressed, was in her early sixties then: handsome, fashionable, urbane, a cigarette always in her hand. She'd just come from the United States, which was much richer in things, including sophistication, in 1952.

As we know from Florence's last chapters in *Fists Upon a Star*, she'd managed to leave Seattle not owing anyone any money. This was amazing, since her theatre had been forced into bankruptcy. Florence owed no one. And, in a spectacular act of denial, Seattle did not think it owed Florence and Burton James. There was no trace of the huge contributions they'd made to civilization in the Pacific Northwest. The slate was wiped clean....

Canada had always seemed poor to Mrs. James. But not now.

I used to come to Canada and they looked awfully
poor to me when I'd come across the border. I used
to be glad that my immigrant parents, grandpar-
ents, had come to the States and not to Canada. I
thought that was an advantage.

And I'd never earned any money really for the-
atre work until I came to Canada, or gotten any
recognition for anything—except maybe a jail sen-
tence—anywhere else....

When Florence immigrated, Saskatchewan did not
yet have full electricity. Farming was the largest industry—family farms run by generations of individuals....

What Saskatchewan *had* though, which was a
remarkable achievement, was an Arts Board. In a truly
dramatic, historical irony, at the same time that the State
of Washington legislature resolved to have an un-American activities committee, Saskatchewan's legislature
voted in favour of an Arts Board....

The James team had made their first appearance in
the province in 1950, two years after the Arts Board's
birth....The 1952 *Annual Report* records:..."The Saskatchewan Arts Board expresses its sincere regret in
reporting the unexpected death...of Mr. Burton James.
The rich contribution he made from his experience of
theatre to the Drama Workshop is deeply appreciated."

Thereafter, Florence James appears permanently,
and alone, in Saskatchewan. She had lost everything, as

Seattle friend Helen Taverniti observed, and yet she was "quite cheerful." Florence had lost her theatre, her life's work, her husband, her reputation, her central place in Seattle society. And yet she is cheerful....

Florence shared some of the memories of her travels [in Saskatchewan] more than twenty years later with me. She didn't drive but travelled by train, and was very proud of her ability to tough out the winters:

> *One of the first things, I'd been teaching summer school and there was a young lady there from Carrot River...And I think she was a minister's wife and she was interested in developing a drama program. I said to Norah [Norah McCullough, then secretary of the Arts Board], "Well I'm off to Carrot River tomorrow."*
>
> *She said, "Oh do you know what it's like up there? They're having a blizzard. You haven't got a fur coat." And I said, "Listen, I wasn't hired 'weather permitting'...."*

...Burton James had observed during their trials that the tragedy of the McCarthy era was "not so much the lives it ruined, but the processes it arrested." He wrestled with how he and Florence could ever possibly resume their valuable work.[16]

Years later, when I met Florence, her one regret was the early death of her husband. She put it simply: Burton could not survive without his theatre building. But Florence got enormous energy and satisfaction from having stood up to and defied the Washington State Committee on Un-American Activities. And she went on to find other venues to exercise her most cherished beliefs. Florence was energized by each Cold War battle, whereas Burton was killed in the McCarthy war. "Florence simply moved their shared ideas and ideals across the border."[17] Mavor Moore discussed her purposeful art in Florence's obituary in the *Globe and Mail*:

Theatre Pioneer Was a Welcome U.S. Invader
"The world will not be saved on the political, military or economic level but on the level of education and art."

Saskatchewan Theatre Pioneer
Florence James (1892–1988)

In Regina tomorrow they will be holding a memorial event for Florence Bean James. She died Jan. 18 at the age of 95. Although she was already past 60 when she arrived in Saskatchewan from Seattle, the news of her death merited a full-page obituary in *The Regina Leader-Post*. But outside of the theatre community, and outside of the West, it appears to have gone unnoticed—perhaps because we've paid very little attention to the phenomenon she personified: the benign American invasion of Canada that accompanied the McCarthy years in the United States.

Florence James was one of the most remarkable of a small group of remarkable women who bullied the performing arts in this country into professionalism, not because she believed in art for art's sake but because she believed the arts have a job to do. She once quoted to me James Baldwin's remark, "Life is more important than art, that's what makes art so important." Born in Idaho and trained in Boston and New York as actor, director and playwright, she reversed the trend and came to Canada to fulfill her ambition. Her ambition was to make human beings, not money.

...She was godmother to the now nationally important Globe Theatre, and to generations of young people who learned to share her social conscience and her love of theatre as its crucible....

There will be those today who see the Florence Jameses as political infiltrators bent on subverting our youth, just as the burghers of Seattle did....They miss the point that she and others like her grasped: that if you want to build human beings, you start with their humanity, not with their color, sex, class, consumer status or political persuasion. You build a society in which humanity can grow....Then you keep working at it, through education and art, until you die.[18]

Since there is no lasting complete record of Florence Bean James versus the Washington State Committee on Un-American Activities (the Canwell Committee, named for its chair), I have combined some transcripts, Florence's recorded memories, and fictionalized scenes into a screenplay, not yet produced. Below is what research and my imagination tell me happened to make the Seattle Repertory Playhouse the target of a witch hunt.

Florence Bean James Being Forcibly Evicted from the Canwell Committee Hearings, 1948 (MOHAI, Seattle Post-Intelligencer Collection, 1986.5.30003.1)

INTERIOR. THE *SEATTLE POST INTELLIGENCER*
EDITOR'S PRIVATE OFFICE—DAY

We can see two areas: a waiting room with four
comfortable chairs and through a glass partition the
editor's desk with two visitors' chairs in front. Al,
thirty-three and cheerful, is in the waiting room. The
EDITOR, mid-fifties, tight suit, balding, and given to
rages, is in his office with ALBERT CANWELL, early
forties, very thin with thinning hair, and his wife,
MRS. CANWELL, early forties, large hat, a foot taller
than Representative Canwell.

>   CANWELL
> Look, I know my committee is supposed to look
> into communistic activities at the University of
> Washington and the Pension Union.

>   MRS. CANWELL
> But we don't think that will garner the amount
> of publicity we all need—Representative
> Canwell needs.

>   EDITOR
> The university is also trying to build a medical
> school, and the Board of Regents asks you to
> take the heat off them.

CANWELL

Not that any of us would think of caving in to
communistic pressure. What about a much
flashier target?

EDITOR

Good idea. But Seattle's got no flash.

CANWELL

Like in Hollywood?
We've got our entertainers and writers too.
We'll be way ahead of Hollywood, ahead of
Washington, ahead of New York!

EDITOR

Right. Our very own Seattle Repertory
Playhouse.

FLORENCE
    (Voice Over, REAL VOICE)
*So this little man by the name of Canwell, and
when I say he was a little man I mean that,
decided that it would be very advantageous if he
could get the money from the legislature to set up
this committee, and he did. This little man said
that there were 150 communists.*

We were called in. Traumatic even remembering it.

INTERIOR. THE SEATTLE ARMORY HEARING
ROOM—DAY

The fake, hastily assembled Hearing Room is ablaze
with light: glaring summer sunlight, newspapers'
flash bulbs, flood lights for newsreels. Representative
Albert Canwell and two young male assistants, bailiffs,
are at the front of the room. Canwell and two other
legislators who are members of his committee are at an
ordinary floor-level wooden table. Canwell frequently
and loudly beats his gavel.

On the "stand," which is a wooden captain's chair to
the right of the table, is GEORGE HEWITT, early
forties, a conservatively dressed, short-haircut,
studious, spectacles-wearing, black, paid witness, the
only witness against Florence James. Audience chairs
are government-issue metal. Florence, Al, Burton,
daughter Marijo, and JOHN CAUGHLAN, their short
and serious civil liberties lawyer, sit in the packed
audience of about 100 AUDIENCE MEMBERS.

>   CANWELL
> Good morning, Ladies and Gentlemen. This
> hearing is necessary, in case you don't read the
> papers, because (*mirthless laugh*) "These are
> times of public danger; subversive persons,
> under cover of the protection afforded by the

bill of rights, seek to destroy our liberties and
our freedom by force, threats and sabotage,
and to subject us to the domination of foreign
powers."

*(Shocked audience reaction during this speech, both
surprise at the announced threats and gasps at the
falsehoods.)*

To quote J. Edgar Hoover, director of the
FBI and a personal hero of mine, "American
Communists have made their deepest inroads
upon our national life. The Communist
influence has projected itself into some
newspapers, books, radio and the screen."

Now to jump right in I will call the witness
George Hewitt. He is a witness against Mrs.
Florence B. James, who is well known in this city
as a director of the Seattle Repertory Playhouse.

HEWITT

Mrs. James is very important in communistic
circles, in fact in the Soviet Union.

CANWELL

Why do you say that, Mr. Hewitt?

HEWITT

I was active in the Communist Party until I
repented. And I know that before leaving for
the Soviet Union Mrs. James was an active
participant in the Seattle Labour School. And
the Washington Pension Union.

CAUGHLAN

Objection! The point of naming these
organizations?

HEWITT

Further, Mrs. James was a supporter of Hugh
Delacey, president of the Washington Commonwealth Federation, in his bids for political office.

CAUGHLAN
(rising to feet)
I object!!! All these groups are open to the
public and legal.

CANWELL
(beating gavel)
Quiet. Lawyers are not part of these proceedings.

HEWITT

Thank you, Mr. Chairman, Representative
Canwell. Continuing with the questionable

activities of Mrs. James, I am sure you are aware
that she has been a candidate for political office
herself, not as successfully as yourself, Sir.

(chuckles)
Running for state senator endorsed by the CIO-
PAC. For those not familiar with these subversive
groups, that is the Congress of Industrial
Organizations-Political Action Committee.

                    CAUGHLAN
I object!!

                    CANWELL
        (beats staccato rhythm)
I am not ejecting you yet, lawyer. But I have
warned.

I know disruptive communistic tactics when I
see them. I did not just ride into town on a hay
wagon.

Lawyers have no place in this hearing.

INTERIOR. A SEATTLE BASEMENT—DAY

Light comes through high basement windows. 200
PEOPLE are in folding chairs and a very heavy,

sad atmosphere. This is Burton James's memorial.
FLORENCE, sixty-two; JACK KINZEL, forty-five;
ALBERTA WALKER, forty-five; and the musician,
Helen Purcell, late forties, address the mourners.
Florence's grandson, JIMMY KINZEL, ten, tries to
comfort her. All are dressed in black or drab. Lots of
AMENS and reactions from the mourners.

                    JACK
We all know that Pop died of a broken heart.
He could survive the Great Depression and a
world war.

He and Mrs. James could survive their firings
from the university's Drama Department.
He survived the unconstitutional witch
hunt of the Washington State Committee on
Un-American Activities.

Is it un-American for our elders to have pensions?

Is it un-American to assert that white and black
people, women and men, should have equal
rights?

But Pop could not survive the theft and brutal
killing of his theatre.

On the last day we owned the Playhouse, Pop
James sat in the audience seats and cried his
heart out. His heart stopped. And he died. Good
night, sweet Prince.

ALBERTA
Amen, Brother Kinzel. Amen, Sister Helen.

And amen to the James family, to daughter
Marijo, little Jimmy, and most of all dear
beloved Mrs. James.

And sympathy for the rest of us. Right. How
much is lost?

At the Playhouse with Mr. and Mrs. James, there
was neither Jew nor Greek. Male nor female.
Slave nor freedman. At the Playhouse, there was
neither black nor white.

Mrs. James, I told you I was going to bring some
religion into this service! That passage from St.
Paul says it.

The Playhouse was the first and only place I was
treated like a person. It did not matter that I am
a Negro.

All I was asked to do was to do my job and do
it well.

Good night, sweet Prince.

We certainly will not rest!

FLORENCE

"A theatre, in the true sense of the word, is a
unity, at the core of which the living community
finds some vital part of itself reflected."

That's what my husband always said and what
we have lived and Burton died by.[19]

The American "invaders" in this section of the book
share an important characteristic: they were involved in
fighting for equality rights for black people, apparently the
signature un-American activity, to such an extent that the
United States either shut them down totally economically
or greatly lessened their life chances. Literally, Florence
James, Grace and Lee Lorch, and Sara Diamond's parents
(whom we are about to meet) were challenged at the pock-
ets. In addition to threatened incomes, their opportunities to pursue the vocations to which they were called, the
work that gave their lives meaning, were threatened.
    In the case of Florence and Burton James specifically,
meaning was completely destroyed. I have included the

fictionalized scene of Burton's funeral because the remaining, and never-again-employed, artists from the Seattle Repertory Playhouse said his life's work was murdered. So was theirs. Burton had decided to come to Canada. That was his hope. However, he was still reporting to a parole officer at the time of his death. Florence said that, even with the hope of a future in Canada at the Banff Centre of the Arts and the Saskatchewan Summer School of the Arts, Burton could not hang on to life.

Meaning, safety, and income were either taken absolutely or greatly threatened for Lee and Grace Lorch, Florence and Burton James, and Jerome and Mary Swit Diamond, the parents of Sara. All of them were sharing meaning and opportunity with people of colour, women, and the working class. These revolutionary political positions made them "un-American." And Florence Bean James was a strong example to me and others thirty years later and beyond.

SARA DIAMOND: WHAT IS TRUTH?

Perhaps at this point the real issue for an adult Sara Diamond is where her mother's storied, remembered, and cherished values have taken her. Her inheritance from her mother makes her a second-generation international countercultural artist and citizen. How much influence does her mother, who died when Sara was very young, have on a mature, honoured, and prestigious Sara? She sees her mother as an important role model in work and life, as a creative artist, as an engaged citizen, and as an arts administrator. The decision to immigrate to Canada from the United States in 1959 was her parents'. Sara was a child at the time. The decision to stay in Canada as a mature adult is hers.

Now president of the Ontario College of Art and Design University, "Canada's university of the imagination," Sara is an award-winning researcher, artist, designer, and scientist, with graduate degrees in Digital Media theory and in Computing, Information Technology and Engineering. She was artistic director of Media and Visual Art and Director of Research at the Banff Centre, where she created the Banff New Media Institute. Today, in her role as president of OCAD University, Sara is guiding her institution towards becoming a leader "in digital media, design research and curriculum through the Digital Futures Initiative, new research in inclusive design, health and design, and sustainable technologies and design."[20]

Sara grew up in a New York Jewish leftist political family that, according to one version, moved to Canada to escape from at least the economic fallout and continued shadows of the McCarthy era. This perhaps made the family economic refugees. What were they to do in the United States for a livelihood and a future? Some family members have remembered these events differently, though, and there is some debate over whether there was an absolute need to escape for safety. Sara is guided by memories of her

heroic mother, shared by her grandmother, both communists who resigned from the party, destroyed the evidence
of their involvement, and certainly did not name names.
Mother wanted to stay in New York and tough it out.
Father felt a compelling need to get away from that past.

Dr. Sara Diamond, President of OCAD University, 2017
(Photo by Martin Iskander)

After completing her university studies in the early
1980s, Sara began to publish actively in various Canadian
art and social history journals. In 1985, she published several articles on cultural politics and feminist ideology in
which she investigated the class positions of artists and
women and their links to the production of culture. In
Diamond's work, her interpretation of the legacy of her

mother, who died when Sara was ten, has been a constant preoccupation, catalyst, inspiration, and source of deep introspection.

Sara believes that the family had to leave New York because of the controversial, activist, revolutionary life of her mother. Mary Swit Diamond was a highly successful social worker who had been active in the Communist Party but had left it after the Khrushchev revelations. According to her paternal grandmother (also a former party member) and her father, her mother had experienced persecution because of her visible politics, prompting his desire and need to leave the United States. Her mother did not intend to create any guilt by association for others.

However, Sara's mother and grandmother believed they had survived the worst of McCarthyism and should remain in the United States. Says Sara:

> Remember, there are two different interpretations of this story, and my mother was not alive for me to ask about it. I was told by my father that my mother had been called up in front of the Committee on Un-American Activities and questioned about her own activities and th[ose] of her colleagues, and my father stated that she did not divulge these.
>
> They had burned their own papers and books to hide evidence of Communist Party membership and involvement. They had left the party by the late 1950s but were

still active on the left. My father was not in the party, not
identified or targeted as my mother was.[21]

Sara's father appears to have thought at the time, 1959–
60, that his wife's activities had greatly compromised his
chances of employment advancement. Canada had those
chances for him. He believed the prospects were bleak
enough in the United States and bright enough in Canada
for the family to move. In this, his experience echoes that
of Florence and Burton James, and Lee and Grace Lorch.

The story from Sara's brother, who is twelve years older,
is that the McCarthy hearings had calmed down. Maybe
the family could have stayed in the city that never sleeps.
According to him, their father thought that he had to leave
the United States strictly for economic reasons. There was
no future for him, though their mother was employed
in a respectable position. Father convinced Mother that
they needed to leave. These differing perceptions were a
source of tension between the couple after their arrival in
Canada, and they sensed that they needed to be somewhat
cautious about their previous political involvements. The
parents' alternative perceptions are part of the siblings'
stories now. Sara has inherited the truth of their fearless
mother, who continued to fight the good socialist fight all
of her short life.

Life had been very exciting for the Diamond family in
that New York scene. Left-leaning celebrities and artists
had come over for breakfast, lunch, dinner, drinks, and

political plans. Sara remembers her little Jewish family as part of the black Harlem Renaissance.

But it couldn't last, said her father. They needed to flee, to go to Canada. Once there, her mother secured good jobs in social services and at the University of Toronto and her father a role as executive director of Jewish Family and Child Services. Although the couple broke ties with their past, they created a new circle of left-leaning former and current communist friends in Canada.[22]

Both parents did well professionally in their new country, but her mother was deeply unhappy in Toronto the Dull. Soon after their move she died, leaving Sara with a rich background for a body of work featuring strong roles for women in all areas of life, including politics. Sara also has had many questions about feminist fearlessness, exile, and solidarity. She has stayed and flourished where she was planted.

Sara has indeed made enormous contributions to the arts in Canada, particularly to feminist arts practice. Through her work as an artist and administrator, she seeks to reverse historical inequities and resource allocations. A program for which she provided substantial support as a co-founder, while heading the Banff New Media Institute, is Women in the Director's Chair (WIDC). Sara recalls that

it was a fantastic moment of convergence. There are times when there's a convergence of vision, and when you get that feeling in your gut you've just got to act!

It was fairly early into my career at Banff, and one of my focuses was getting creative work and artists onto [television] programs.

We were very conscious of the small number of women actually making their way into directing feature films and television. Looking at what was happening in some other countries, like Australia and [the] UK, there was a concerted effort on the part of women to create specific training programs, learning opportunities, boot camps outside of college or university programs with funding from the governments of those countries. To be successful in those commercial/competitive worlds of feature films and television (or just broadcast), we wanted to offer these kinds of opportunities to Canadian women.[23]

Sara, Carol Whiteman, the founding producer and continuing CEO, and Peg Campbell, faculty member at Emily Carr, realized that, combined, they had the resources to begin one solution to a big problem. They were all concerned about the minuscule number of women filling key creative chairs in film and television: producer, director, writer, lead actor—these roles were seldom occupied by women. The WIDC founders knew that women in charge would create a different type of story, a different working environment, and a different product on the screen. Together they could create a unique opportunity for women to learn, to grow, to produce. So Women in the

Director's Chair was born at Banff. Whiteman, Campbell, and Diamond seized the moment of convergence, and the resulting program has lasted more than twenty years.[24]

In her work, Sara has constantly put herself and others at the leading edge. Those others are frequently women, Indigenous and visible minority people, and marginalized artists. She works to move these individuals and groups into the mainstream, where their perspectives can be heard, felt, and made useful.

When Sara was named one of the fifty most influential people in Toronto in 2014, she was described as "a woman ahead of her time."[25] Perhaps Sara inherited that trait, since her mother was also a highly visible revolutionary in her work. In fact, Mary Swit Diamond was sufficiently well known that *The New York Times* reported on her death five years after she moved to Toronto.[26]

Sara's 1982 resonant videotape *The Influences of My Mother* positions her mother in relation to political struggles and in a love-questioning relationship with Sara. Curator Jean Gagnon explored these ideas in his essay from the exhibition catalogue for the National Gallery of Canada's 1992 exhibition *Sara Diamond: Mémoires Ravivées, Histoire Narrée / Memories Revisited, History Retold*:

> In Diamond's works, historical knowledge is sought in order to determine what parts of the past are still reflected in the present; it is simultaneously called into question because the past, strictly speaking, remains

unknowable, albeit inescapable....It is thus an imaginary recognition....

In *The Influences of My Mother* (1982), Diamond explores her relationship with her mother, who died when Diamond was ten years old. Through family snapshots of her mother, to whom she bears a striking resemblance, the artist confronts both her mother, who is physically absent and made "doubly" absent by the iconic "presence" of the photographs, and her own identity....

In this tape, Sara Diamond is both narrator and director; her tone is at times tender and at times filled with rage toward this absent mother....

Toward the end of the tape, in the section dealing with the Heroic Mother, Diamond makes known her mother's political involvement with New York labour unions.[27]

In the present, Sara is left with a strong political feminist role model of a mother. That is the mother whom she remembers and cherishes. Perhaps it is not important how other members of the family view her mother's history. Sara views her own work as exploring not only the direct influences of her mother but also the era and its significance.

Sara is left in a Canada that has supported and fostered her alternative, feminist, visual arts practice. She thinks that her practice would have been the same wherever she lived, the United States, Canada, or elsewhere. However, support for that practice, and other opportunities to be an intellectual trailblazer, might be uniquely Canadian and nurtured by the Canada of the 1960s–80s.

Sara's critique of Canada is most visible in the way that OCAD University is evolving. For example, OCAD has recently responded to the Calls to Action in the report of the Truth and Reconciliation Commission—particularly the Commission's call to "integrate Indigenous knowledge and teaching methods into classrooms"[28]—by making "decolonization number one on its list of six priorities guiding its academic planning through 2022."[29] These initiatives by OCAD University were featured in Chris Rattan's 2017 *NOW* magazine article entitled "The plan to decolonize design":

> Decolonization is a faculty-wide initiative [at OCAD], and while it's clear how Eurocentrism has dominated English, history and art, what about subjects presumed neutral? How do you decolonize science? How do you decolonize design?
>
> When OCAD began its search for a new dean of its Faculty of Design two years ago, decolonization was in the job description. It's what attracted Dori Tunstall to the role. She's the first Black woman dean of a design faculty anywhere in the world. She recalls a recent lecture in London where her status as the world's-only was met with a round of applause. "Really?" she laughs. "But it's 2017."…

"It's about shifting demographics. The fastest-grow-
ing population in Canada is the Indigenous population;
the other growing population is through immigration,"
[Tunstall] says.…"If future students do not see themselves
in these practices, they will not go to these universities.[30]

Sara is definitely leading the venerable high-art institution in some different directions: decolonization, digital arts, diversity. (We'll meet Sara's dean of the Faculty
of Design, Dori Tunstall, and this book's most recent
American refugee in Chapter 5.)

Sara did not choose to immigrate to Canada, but she
did choose to remain in Canada, challenging and shaping the story here and now. A huge part of her mature
work has been giving voice to those *left out* of our national
openness, including women in liberation movements. In
the 2000s, this marginalized majority group might not
have made as much progress in Canada as it did in prior
decades. Consider the continued struggle for equal pay
for work of equal value, sexual harassment in major institutions, and the fact that there are still too few women on
boards or in key creative positions.[31]

Sara said goodbye to her 100-year-old father in 2016.
She is deeply appreciative of the gifts that her parents gave
her, including coming to Canada and a rich history of
fighting against social injustice and supporting marginalized people. For Sara, one of the great things about moving to Canada is support for the arts, public education,

and affordable public institutions to which all Canadians can have access.

Sara has been a part of or led some of these institutions, including the Emily Carr School of Design, the Banff New Media Centre, and now OCAD University. Of more significance are the agendas that she has been able to advocate and foster in those institutions: interdisciplinary knowledge, diversity, equal opportunity for minorities, gender equality, and Indigenous rights. This inheritance, too, is from her parents.

What worries Sara most about the present era? The erosion of support for the arts, education, and public institutions, of course. And how innovative Canada will be in making the transition from a resource-based economy to the creative economy. These are worrisome realities and questions for her.

For those caught up in the right-wing Cold War chill of the McCarthy era in the United States, Canada was a much better country. Yet it had its own Cold War at the time, largely comprised of attacks on cultural institutions. For instance, the NFB and the CBC experienced purges of suspected communist sympathizers, and the chill reappeared at various moments. When Canadians can admit that history, they will be on their way to making a much better country.

When immigrants from the United States are established in Canada, they often remain activists. They question not only their own pasts that brought them here

but also the present state of Canadian society. This phenomenon has been researched most extensively among
Vietnam War resisters, some of whom we will meet in
the next chapter, but it characterizes expats in all waves of
immigration from the United States to Canada. Those who
decided to stay where it was cold and lonely made serious individual commitments and contributions to their
adopted country.

FOUR

FACES TURNED TOWARD CANADA
VIETNAM WAR RESISTERS

More words in books and more minutes on air have been created about the Vietnam War resisters (dodgers, deserters, etc.) than about any other wave of immigrants from the United States to Canada. This is likely because many of the resisters landed in image-producing industries: publishing, journalism, media, and universities. They comprised the most recent "invasion" prior to 2006, so it is also in the lived experiences and memories of many Canadians.

In his 2001 book *Northern Passage: American Vietnam War Resisters in Canada*, John Hagan calls the migration

of more than 50,000 draft-age American men and women
to Canada during the Vietnam War "the largest politically motivated exodus from the United States since the
country's beginnings," and he asks, "Was [this movement]
simply a marginal, highly individualized spin-off of the
American antiwar movement?…Or…did the exile migration have its own original, organized, and lasting collec-
tive meaning?"[1]

The meta-story/legend is relatively simple and mem-
orable. Canada welcomed those fleeing an immoral war
and provided them with great opportunities. Jessica
Squires's *Building Sanctuary: The Movement to Support
Vietnam War Resisters in Canada, 1965–73* points out that
this story we love to tell ourselves is not totally accurate.
The complete story is more nuanced. Canada was not in
direct combat in Vietnam, but it had many infrastructure
involvements in the Vietnam War. And recently, refugee
advocate Mary Jo Leddy commented on Canada's role in
that war and the difficulties our preferred story causes us:

> We have developed what I would call a "branch plant
> morality" that puts the blame for wrongs at the head
> office which is always elsewhere, anywhere but here.
> It is a dangerous innocence and blinds us to the very
> real good that we are capable of and the evil that we can
> manage on our own. For example, we protested mightily
> against the conduct of the American government during
> the Viet Nam war but didn't notice that Agent Orange

was being produced in the lovely little town of Elmira, Ontario. Our myth of innocence not only blinds us to the evil we are capable of but to the very real goodness that exists within the heart of America itself.[2]

In addition, at the federal level Canada needed to support its biggest ally and trading partner and was not completely welcoming to the resisters. Nonetheless, many were welcomed.[3] They were white, young, well-educated, and fluent English speakers. What was not to like about these immigrants?

MY STORY CONTINUES: THE UNITED STATES, A GOOD COUNTRY TO LEAVE

Because I am female, I can't claim to be a Vietnam War draft resister. Plus, I am black, and very few of this wave of immigration were non-white. I look with interest, however, at my own crossing of the border in the same years, 1967–68, as the individuals profiled in this chapter. They have all pointed out that the centennial year was a stellar time to come to Canada: a proud, confident country sure of its place in the world as enlightened, peaceable, and sophisticated. Canada needed well-educated, English-speaking (and sometimes French-speaking or willing to learn), motivated new immigrants who would move anywhere.

The plain truth is that I immigrated to Canada in 1967 because I married a Canadian. There were many such marriages in that era: Canadian women who married Vietnam War resisters to make it easy for them to immigrate; marriages of convenience that usually just lapsed, as planned, when the mission was accomplished; American couples who quickly got married to facilitate their immigration, some of whom have remained activist Canadian power teams to the present; and some marriages breaking up, with one partner remaining in Canada and the other returning to the United States when that was possible.

In retrospect, what is interesting to me about my own case is how easy it was to say, after four weeks of knowing Rex Deverell, "Yes, I will leave everything I have known and immigrate to a different country." The obvious explanation is that his overwhelming charm, talent, wit, good looks, spirituality, and brilliance swept me off my feet! Fifty years later and somewhat more clear-eyed, I have no doubt that these attractive characteristics account for why we are still married, through his appointment as playwright-in-residence at Regina's Globe Theatre to subsequent work in St. Thomas, Toronto, Winnipeg, and Halifax. Worth examining with hindsight, though, is how easy it was to leave a country whose economy had been based upon the enslavement of people with my African ancestry, and that was waging a war that so many of my generation thought immoral, at the height of the Civil Rights movement and consciousness.

The ease with which I said "yes" is recounted in *Smoked Glass Ceiling*:

SCENE #4 June 19, 1967

During the first week of graduate school, 1966—New York City still—everything has turned even more wonderful and I realize it.

I'm standing at the bulletin board.

And this guy—who turns out to be Canadian—asks to borrow a text book about ritual, theatre and religions.

He never leaves my side after that. Four weeks later, standing in the shelter of the public wash rooms on the Hudson River, he says "It's colder than this in Canada. Why don't you marry me?"

Actually he didn't know about cold yet, being from balmy Ontario. That was way before he'd even been to Regina and Winnipeg, where we've lived.

But I digress. There is a great deal of freedom in mating for life. Freedom to build, to create, to grow, to fly a distance from your rich hive, to think, to explore ideas, until your safe return. The slavery of looking for someone to love you every two weeks or so goes away—if you're lucky.[4]

It was a remarkably easy decision to ditch the United States. Thinking back on it now, I recall that shortly before our wedding Rex said, "Maybe we should stay here in New York." Like many Canadians then and since, he found the glitter of the United States attractive. I quickly vetoed this notion and happily moved from the eight million people of Manhattan to the 23,000 of St. Thomas, Ontario. The transition was a big culture shock in many ways. But it was totally easy for a black girl from the American South, in a country in the middle of wars both at home and in Southeast Asia, to see it as a good move. Plus Rex, growing up in Orillia, had read to me aloud from Stephen Leacock's *Sunshine Sketches of a Little Town* so that I'd understand the central mythology of that most cherished of Canadian folksy images. Mariposa sounded terrific. That was, of course, long before I had to worry about Leacock's "dark side" as a possible "misogynist racist."[5]

The "American refugees" whom we meet below have been remarkable professionals and activists and major contributors to our national well-being and esteem. They have also voiced critiques of Canada. These individuals seem, at first glance, to fit the positive story perfectly. Canada welcomed these war resisters. All of them were called in different ways to continue their activism in Canada. One was on the East Coast; two were on the West Coast; two were in Toronto. But first we meet one resister who found his haven and his career in the unique social democratic government of Saskatchewan in the 1970s.

CRAIG DOTSON: WE CAME
AS IMMIGRANTS, NOT EXILES

When Rex and I moved to Regina in 1971, friends from Toronto said, "You must meet the Dotsons in Saskatchewan. Craig and Kathy had a temporary home in our Annex house after they immigrated. Craig was a Vietnam draft resister. Of course, they had no family in Canada. They'd left the US with nothing." After I got to know Craig and Kathy, I did audiotaped interviews (never published, never broadcast) with Craig in the 1980s. What

Craig Dotson and Son Allan (Dotson family photo)

follows is taken from those interviews and from insights shared with me in 2017 by one of the Dotsons' adult children. The last time I'd spoken to Allan Dotson, he was a child. Now over forty, he is the middle child of Craig and Kathy. He was always part of a bouncing welcome of Dotson children at their annual Boxing Day reception when we lived in Regina in the 1970s.

Allan told me that he can't remember a time when he didn't know his father was a Vietnam War resister. The complexity of his parents' story evolved for Allan as he got older. Two factors have shaped his memories of his father and his own adult philosophy: Craig's resistance to war and his deep dedication to the social democratic government of Saskatchewan.

Allan, a comic book writer and teacher, had an opportunity to memorialize his father's legacy. In 2012, four years after his father's death, Allan was one of the artists-in-residence to celebrate the 100th anniversary of the Saskatchewan legislature. "The Leg." is the building where Craig spent the majority of his working life. Each artist created a legacy artwork to be installed in one of the eight alcoves of the rotunda.

Allan shared with me a long letter that Craig had written to his three children at Christmas time in 2006, four years after his beloved wife Kathy's death in 2002. The letter was entitled "Family Matters" and in it Craig recalled the circumstances and thinking that had led to their move from the US to Canada:

Comic Strip by Allan Dotson, Rotunda of the Saskatchewan Legislative Building, 2012 (Courtesy of Allan Dotson)

From the US military perspective, the Vietnam War was going badly. The ostensible and official South Vietnamese leaders were untrustworthy, incompetent, corrupt, and indistinguishable. Ho Chi Minh was an effective and highly respected political leader in the North, his top general, Giap, was brilliantly success- ful, and the Viet Cong had great support across South Vietnam and seemed unbeatable. In the US, domestic opposition to the war was growing wider and deeper. Universal male conscription was less and less popular, and ordinary families began to tolerate or encourage their sons to get a draft deferment—by studies, mar- riage, or any other means.

One began to read more often about "draft dodgers," and not always negatively.[6]

For Allan, the resister legacy was definitely not nega- tive. It was a proud history. It was the family's origin story, as Craig's letter explains:

As I returned to Tucson in September 1967 to begin what I knew would be my final undergraduate semester and thus the certain end of my student draft deferment, I began paying a lot closer attention to all of this….I had a very satisfying independent reading course on Early Modern France. It was then that I determined to focus any subsequent graduate study on the Enlightenment and the French Revolution. Much more importantly, [I was] recommended to a colleague at Queen's University in Canada. My smallest, most difficult and most rewarding class, though, was the European Intellectual History seminar. One of my classmates was a charming, intelligent, beautiful and delightful Art History major, Kathy Kenyon.

Craig and Kathy had intellectual and artistic interests in common. As with most American citizens of draftable age, the Vietnam War soon loomed in their consciousness and interrupted their love story:

We began to figure out how to plan for a life together.... She had done very well in Studio Art and in her Art History major and was planning to pursue her doctorate at Indiana. I wanted to pursue my own doctorate in French History. But the end of my draft deferment was coming...as I would graduate at the end of the first semester, in late January.

The more I learned about southeast Asia, the US involvement and its stated goals, and the more closely I followed the political and military conflict—the more deeply became my conviction that the US position was immoral. I thought its purposes had much more to do with Cold War US geopolitics than with the well-being of the Vietnamese people. I wanted the North Vietnamese to win, to unite their own country to live as a single sovereign nation, free from the colonial presence of the French or the neo-colonial presence of the US.

This strong objection to the actual war in Vietnam is significant in Craig's story. Those who came to Canada only to lead a more pleasant life and to avoid the draft have little to talk about fifty years later. For the five resisters profiled in *American Refugees*, however, fleeing the United States was a crucial and clarifying decision in their lives. It determined their moral, ethical, and political attitudes throughout adulthood and into their senior years. Craig's letter explains the evolution of his own stance and response to the war at this time:

> For a couple of months I convinced myself that I was really a circumstantial pacifist, and applied for "conscientious objector" status with the Draft Board. I was obviously not a Quaker, and the status I sought would entail my being drafted, but serving in the field without bearing arms, e.g., as a medic. I obtained three letters of support....By the time the notice arrived advising me that my request had been granted, however, my position had changed and hardened, and I became determined not to serve in that army during that war. And thus amidst all of our other personal and academic preoccupations that winter, we began to prepare for my departure. We had decided on Canada. Everyone who knew of my plans was respectful, accepting of my decision, and supportive.
>
> One of those older married graduate students from my American History class became a special friend for

a brief time. He and his wife were about ten years older than us. They invited us to their home for a wonderful evening of good company and their delicious green corn tamales. He was at the time a major in the US Air Force, and was the commanding officer at one of the ICBM silo sites, each with a nuclear armed rocket aimed at the USSR, that ringed Tucson. He was from Ajo, a small mining town near the Mexican border. When he learned of my plans to emigrate to Canada, he gave me the name and contact information for a school and college friend of his, Les McLean, also from Ajo, now living in Toronto.

Rex and I met Dr. Les and Mrs. Ellen McLean in 1968 when we billeted them in our first Canadian apartment in St. Thomas. We didn't know then about the upcoming wedding of Craig and Kathy in Toronto. Craig's letter recalls the stress and uncertainty of that time for him and Kathy. And, like many others in any wartime, their personal situation lives in a national and international context:

Until I received the draft notice, and then failed to show up as called, I would be committing no crime or offense. But we were all apprehensive nonetheless. We decided that I would leave at the beginning of March, find work in Toronto until the fall, Kathy would join me upon her graduation in June, and we would then get married. In September we would move to Kingston which we thought was not too terribly far from Toronto, [and] I would pursue my PhD at Queen's. And we would live happily ever after.

Remarkably, almost all of that turned out exactly as planned. I remained for a month after graduation. Entering Canada was not too difficult. Upon my telling the Canadian border authorities my intention to emigrate, they took me and my suitcases off the bus at 3:00 a.m., accepted my then-and-there application for Landed Immigrant status, and put me back on the next bus to Toronto a few hours later.

That was a very full spring. Within a three month period, I found a data processing job in Toronto, connected with Les and Ellen McLean and moved into their basement, President Johnson announced that the US would stop bombing Hanoi, Martin Luther King was assassinated, Robert Kennedy was assassinated. Czechoslovakia, and the French student movement took over Paris in its May Revolution. In late June Pierre Trudeau fought and won his first election as Liberal Leader and Prime Minister.

Although it seems remarkable now, Craig and Kathy had not realized that he could not return to the United States to get married. So their plan changed a bit:

Then in late June we got married. As it turned out, my status meant that I could not return to the US without risk of arrest as a fugitive felon (draft evasion in the US was a felony), so we had to get married in Toronto. A small wedding: no one from my family; Kathy's parents and one aunt and one of her college friends; Ellen McLean and her delightful daughters Bonnie and Adina (Les phoned the night before from his business trip to Venezuela); and a couple of my work colleagues. I think we got ten wedding presents. Three were toasters.

As a very welcome wedding present Kathy's parents gave us a six-year-old vw beetle, which Tom had cleaned up and tuned. Our three-day honeymoon trip eastward to Kingston and the Thousand Islands had only two awkward bits. Those old vws did not have a fuel gauge display, and an hour and a half after leaving our wedding reception, in mid-afternoon, along the 401 towards Kingston, we ran out of gas. The following afternoon, part way through the cruise among the Thousand Islands, I was terrified to realize that we were, for a few minutes, cruising through us waters. When the boat stopped on some particularly scenic island inside New York state and we were invited to walk around and take pictures, I stayed on board and tried to become invisible. Being a fugitive felon was OK. I did not want to be an apprehended one.

In my recorded conversations with Craig, made some twenty years before he wrote the "Family Matters" letter to his children, he stressed that the decision to stay in Canada, to become Canadians, was made before his departure from the United States. He and Kathy knew from the beginning that they were not just intending to escape across the border and return to their old lives when it was safe. There was only one choice for Craig and Kathy.

The year was 1967, the new age of super-patriotism in the United States. The country would not allow the people of Southeast Asia to become communists. It would send young men of draft age to be killed in an unwinnable war against an unclear enemy. Black Americans did not see the problem: "No Vietnamese ever called me nigger" was a popular slogan of the day. Many white Americans did not see the problem either, and Craig was one of them. He wanted to go to graduate school, marry Kathy, have children, and lead a socially productive life.

Hundreds of thousands of young American citizens wanted what he wanted. When the decision was made, it was astonishingly easy. Craig would not bear arms in Southeast Asia. As a conscientious objector, he would not heal the wounded in Southeast Asia so that they could fight again. As he mentioned in our recorded conversation,

> I was not convinced that imposing from the bellies of
> B-52s the American way of life on Vietnam peasants was
> going to make their lives any better. And obviously I was
> intensely and personally interested in what would happen
> to me when I graduated. Draft resistance had not yet
> begun on any large scale, at least in Arizona, much more
> so around Berkeley, much more so around New Haven.

The possibility of going underground occurred to me for just a moment but had no appeal whatsoever. We toyed in the most cursory fashion with immigrating to Cuba.

I decided I would not go and participate in that war...arms bearing or otherwise. And quite quickly then, because I anticipated the draft notice, I anticipated that I might be drafted within six weeks, and as it turned out I was quite accurate in that prediction.

So after about four weeks I left, took the bus to Chicago, where I first met my prospective in-laws and told them I was going to marry their daughter and take her away to a foreign country.[7]

Nineteen sixty-eight was a vintage year for leaving the United States. Craig had been living in the Toronto "Y" only for a few weeks when parts of his old world started to crumble and burn. It was a good year to immigrate. Expatriates huddled in groups north of the border if they were exiles. More likely they stood singly and tried to figure out their new country if they were immigrants. And both groups wondered what had happened to the United States that they had left. It seemed to be going crazy:

I had been in Canada about a week. Three major things happened while I was staying in the YMCA. This would be March 1968.

Martin Luther King was shot.

Bobby Kennedy was shot.

And Johnson made his announcement that he was going to stop the bombing of North Vietnam and not seek re-election.

Craig watched with a mixture of enormous grief, unbelievable embarrassment, and cosmic relief that it was no longer his country. For him, the possible end to the war in Vietnam did not signal that it was time to go home. Home had moved. The United States was no longer home.

While we came to Canada with all negative feelings and no positive ones, we came at the very outset as immigrants and not as exiles. And for us that was a distinction we made from the very beginning and made it resolutely and stuck to it.

It had an important impact on us because in Toronto for the first four months there was a sizable, active, vocal exile community. And they published anti-war newsletters, and they had little meetings and speeches and marches and so on. It was always my impression from a distance that they were exiles, not immigrants.

I didn't want to be an exile. I wanted to become a Canadian. This was my new country. So from the very outset Kathy and I turned our back on the United States, turned our face to Canada to become Canadians. And the only thing that caught our interest really ever again about American affairs was Watergate. We never did follow American affairs, never went to a protest march, never went to a draft dodgers' meeting or whatever. And at Queen's there were fewer draft Americans. There were three or four, but we had little to do with them because by that time, over the years, we just became more and more interested in learning about our new country and becoming part of it.

And so, while all the emotions on the day I crossed the border were negative ones and not a positive attraction to Canada, within a very short time it was quite the contrary. It was a whole host of positive reasons for staying here. The negative feelings sort of died down and diminished in their intensity. Now I feel on a scale of 1 to 100 that my intensity of positive feelings about Canada is 99, but my intensity of negative feelings for the United States [is] way down, at the bottom of the scale.

I no longer have a lot of negative vibrations about me and the US. I mean, it's a country like a lot of others. It's not my country.

Craig came to Canada at a moment when immigrants like him were welcomed. It was the year of the centennial. Canada could do anything. Later, it became more diffi cult to immigrate. A potential immigrant had to have a sponsor. An immigrant had to have a job. The Canada of 1967–68 was, for the most part, a confident, secure, sane place welcoming those from insane environments. Craig described to me his experience in crossing the border:

I said I want to [im]migrate to Canada. So he took me and my suitcase off, sent the bus on its way, took me into his little shack, and we filled out all the forms, and that was the date of my application. I had no job, not even the prospect of a job, nor any place to stay in Toronto. And after that it was all very mechanical and very simple. I mean that was the only intense moment of any consequence. That's when I filled out all the forms, and they gave me the number of points that you get for being healthy or single or educated or having a job skill in demand.

Then Kathy came up in June. She registered to be an immigrant at that time, and we became citizens at the earliest possible opportunity, five years later, 1973. It was easier for her still because she was marrying a person who was already a landed immigrant. And, within two or three months of my arrival in Canada, I was accepted at Queen's for graduate work and was awarded a teaching assistantship. So that was a nice welcoming gesture on the part of Canada.

The other thing about our experience as newcomers to Canada was really blessed from the beginning in so many ways. In 1968, there was essentially what we would look back on nostalgically as full employment. Getting a job was easy. I walked the streets of Toronto for three weeks very despondent as I read the newspaper ads every day, and three weeks later I had a job. And that was just off the bus.

The United States had carried the Cold War all the way to Vietnam. On the one hand, the United States was still fighting. On the other, Canada had quietly buried its Cold War and its Cold War dead. Assistance to the United States and its causes did exist, but at a high federal level. Cooperating with their southern neighbour didn't touch ordinary Canadian citizens much. The purge of the National Film Board was complete. Real or perceived dissidents no longer cluttered up Ottawa.

> It was a good time for us too because of when I entered Canadian graduate school. In 1968, the Canada Council and the federal government and universities were into a major, major expansion campaign to train new PhDs to staff the growing universities. And I sort of came at the beginning of that. A lot of money for scholarships, a lot of money for teaching assistantships. And our graduate student days, while not lush by any means, were certainly very comfortable in an economic sense.

In 1971, Craig completed his doctorate. He could become a professor of history, have a family, and live a productive and happy life with Kathy. There was only one difficulty: Canada no longer needed professors of history. Craig didn't consider going back to the United States or emigrating to another country. He was now a Canadian. And a staunch, dedicated, activist Canadian he remained until his death.

After a lot of reflection, Craig decided to become a public servant. He had come to see Canada as a better society than the one from which he had come:

> Things like medical care insurance and hospitalization and some of the social programs that were so obviously there for us as Ontario residents. The bilingual nature of the country. The fact that it was known throughout the world as a peacekeeper rather than a warmonger. All of these things gave us pride in being Canadian, rather than shame, compared to us as Americans. We felt pride in now being Canadian and being part of this. We had moved from a country without Medicare and OHIP to a country with Medicare.
>
> I was anxious and unhappy and stewing for several months until I reached the conclusion that I would take a course in public administration and enter the public service. I did so out of an old-fashioned sense of public service. One is told that sense existed in the best years of the British public service, in India and the home service. One is told it existed in the early years after the war in Canada.
>
> Then in the fall of '75 I began looking around for work....I knew very well that there was a New Democratic government in British Columbia, in Saskatchewan, and in Manitoba. I was bilingual. I had always assumed, in that central Ontario way that Queen's people have, that I would find work in the federal public service where being bilingual would be an asset.

But in that public administration program I learned a lot more. And everywhere I went I kept hearing, "Well, in Saskatchewan of course, if you want to work there, that's the best there is. First, you know, there is the federal public service, but if you really want to do something interesting there's this little, tiny, elite civil service in Saskatchewan." It prized energy, ability, and clear thinking, and it was not afraid to recruit the best and the brightest from Queen's or wherever else. And wanted to make use of them as sharp, keen-edged tools as it went about its way doing good in Saskatchewan. I knew nothing about what doing good in Saskatchewan was all about.

I was looking for really the most interesting career challenge, but I was not at all unimpressed with the fact that a social democratic government in a province with a history of social democratic government was the place for me. And I turned down a couple of offers in Ottawa. They weren't particularly interesting, and the size of the Ottawa bureaucracy just dismayed me. I was just overwhelmed when I saw it from the windows of the train.

I was charmed and quite taken by the fascinating job opportunity I had in Saskatchewan working with the Secretariat to the Treasury Board in the Budget Bureau, about which I knew little. I was hired in May of 1975 and arrived here a month after the 1975 election, which returned the Blakeney government.

So I came as a New Democrat, but I came first as a professional public servant. I would have happily gone

to work for the Ontario government had they offered
me something that I found a challenge and interesting
in a place that I would learn a lot. But I was particularly
happy to be coming, not so much to the west, but it was
the prospect of working in what was thought elsewhere
to be the best public service in Canada.

Craig felt increasingly comfortable with his growing
awareness that this elite public service had been developed
from a precise set of social goals. It was a completely different and totally satisfying society for him. His personal
agenda was the same as his society's agenda. This was a
new experience for him:

I knew enough of the achievements of the Douglas years
and enough about the stature of Blakeney as a person to
know that, whatever their goals were, I would be pleased
to help fulfill them. It was only after I arrived here that
I developed a sense of understanding of Saskatchewan
or a sense of what a great place Saskatchewan was or
why the New Democrats, the CCF, the tradition seems to
fit so well, and why it seemed to have been particularly
well-suited to achieve some of the traditions.

For me, the major social conclusions I drew were,
first, that the province was incredibly vulnerable to
power from abroad, Toronto or the CPR or Denver or
Johannesburg, and second, the historical way of the people over time and the New Democrat way of the 1970s to

cope with that was to do whatever possible to become masters in one's own house.

Craig's proudest achievement as a civil servant, at the time we talked, was the design of a new Workers' Compensation plan. Craig was then a senior adviser in the Department of Labour. He had experience with what an industrial accident could do to a family with low or middle income. He had learned about the social benefits of Workers' Compensation as a boy. He was able, as a Saskatchewan civil servant, to make life better for all of the working people of the province. Saskatchewan provided Craig in the 1970s and 1980s with a way to contribute to the overall quality of life for its people.

A Regina *Leader-Post* tribute to Craig Dotson following his death in 2008 summarized how Saskatchewan was a haven of sanity and productivity for him and his family:

Leader-Post September 10, 2008

REGINA Being a lifelong learner who loved to share knowledge made Craig Dotson well-suited to his 10-year post as deputy minister of learning beginning in the mid-1990s.

"He was a person who taught…," said James Burton, who worked with Dotson in the NDP caucus office.

"He was enthusiastic. He wanted to see young people active and aware of politics. It was a passion for him. Craig

believed in 'the New Jerusalem'; he believed in a better
world and that the way to do that was through politics."[8]

War resister Dr. Craig Dotson had gained enormously
from immigrating to Canada. And he had given back
equally, by giving to Saskatchewan a balanced budget as
deputy minister of finance and through his distinguished
service as the deputy of both the Ministry of Learning and
the Ministry of Education. And in retirement he'd spread
his knowledge.

To his son Allan, Craig bequeathed a name, that of
Allan Blakeney, the NDP premier of Saskatchewan from
1971 to 1982 and one of Craig's role models. Craig also
bequeathed the idea of public service and using one's
gifts and resources to enrich the lives of others. In Allan's
career as a comic book designer, a recent project was to
coach elementary school students in the creation of a
comic strip about the Syrian refugee crisis. Welcome to
the Saskatchewan of the Dotsons.

I speculate that, if Craig and Kathy were alive now,
they might be very involved in the War Resisters League,
Vietnam War survivors who encourage the Canadian
government to welcome and stop deporting Iraq War
resisters. They might also encourage Saskatchewan and
Manitoba to welcome the asylum seekers who in many
cases have travelled across three or four continents to get
to Canada. After all, the Prairies remain a vast and sparsely
populated region that needs particularly determined and

hard-working people willing to address the inequitable treatment of Indigenous peoples. That is only speculation, of course, about some of the issues the Dotsons might have been working on in 2018.

ED MILLER: LIFELONG WAR RESISTER

Dr. Joanne Tompkins is chair of the Department of Curriculum and Instruction at St. Francis Xavier University in Antigonish, Nova Scotia. She quipped in 2014, while smiling impishly, that her late husband, Ed Miller, was so good at running an Inuit-based education program in Cape Dorset, Nunavut, that she married him.[9]

Tragically, Ed died of cancer while he still had a beloved young family, children aged seven and eleven. Those children are now young adults, and Joanne says that she and her children are continuing Ed's legacy of activism, protest, and making their immediate world a better place. Ed's obituary describes his life and legacy:

Ed Miller, father, brother, friend, activist, psychotherapist and educator, died peacefully at home on Monday, July 21, 2003, surrounded by his loving family. His battle with cancer over the past few months was filled with the same determination, courage and community activism that characterized the rest of his life. A passionate intellectual with wide and varied interests, Ed lived what he believed[,] beginning with the civil rights movement and including extensive work with anti-war, anti-poverty, anti-racism, disability rights and union labour organizations. He inspired, influenced and touched all who knew him. Born in New York in 1948,...he moved to Canada as a young man to continue resisting the war in Vietnam.[10]

Dr. Joanne Tompkins, 2017 (Miller-Tompkins family photo)

The family's commitment to that legacy is evident in their request that donations in memory of Ed be sent to the National Anti-Poverty Organization.

When I approached Joanne about this book, she welcomed the opportunity to detail many of Ed's social justice commitments during their years in Antigonish, and much of what follows here is her own writing. She describes this act of writing as a "bittersweet journey," but she says it is a journey that was long overdue and one which she had intended to take for her children and herself. She begins with Ed's formative New York upbringing, rich in political activity and social awareness, lived in love and poverty:

> Both sides of Ed's family were involved in trade unions. Many Jewish immigrants who arrived in New York in the early 1920s worked in the garment industry and became active members of unions which brought about significantly safer and better working conditions for the members. Unionism remained a strong thread of the fabric of Ed's life.
>
> In 1953 (father) Charles was having minor routine surgery performed and died as a result of some unexpected complications....This was a sad, sudden, and life-changing event for Ed's family. Left with few resources and two small children, (mother) Marion was forced to move from their recently purchased starter home into public housing. In the early 1950s public housing in [the] Bedford-Stuyvesant area of Brooklyn consisted of 8-storey buildings with almost no common or green spaces provided. African Americans and Latinos made up most of the population of the public

housing projects on Sutter Avenue where Ed lived most
of his years in Brooklyn. The Millers were one of only a
few white families in the projects and Ed recalled often
being the only white student in the public schools he
attended.

Ed's initial orientation to equity and justice were
formed against this family, cultural and community
backdrop. Living in the "projects" he experienced firsthand the classism aimed at families there by municipal
governments and organizations whose missions were to
"help the poor."[11]

By 1967, it had become too dangerous for Ed, who was
of draftable age, to stay in the United States. As a war pro-
tester he risked possible imprisonment, which would not
do the war resister movement any good.

On February 5, 1967 Ed boarded a train and headed
north. We know the exact date because at 12:05 am on
February 5, 1992, 25 years from the day he arrived in
Canada, his daughter, Marion, was born. Like so many
Americans of the time Ed, just having turned 19, packed
quickly and headed north, having little idea of what lay
beyond the American border.

Although his life didn't instantly sort itself out when he
arrived in Canada, Ed was able for the next thirty-six years
to support the causes that he thought just and important.

Joanne remembers that

for many years Ed was not allowed to enter the United
States. Although there were several clemencies granted
to war evaders (i.e. President Carter, 1977) and war resisters, Ed's name was never struck from that list and he died
without having been reinstated as an American citizen.

Joanne continues the story by quoting from Roger
Neville Williams's *The New Exiles: American War Resisters
in Canada*:

The Vancouver Committee served as a model for the
Montreal Council to Aid War Resisters....These groups
had little radical foundation and were merely intended
to be of assistance to young men who were in desperate
need of help, but Ed Miller brought a little more radical
consciousness to the Montreal Council when he arrived
early in 1967. Miller had come from New York where he
had worked with the group of early resisters....[12]

Ed was one of those who left the United States with
nothing, who had no connections in Canada yet was able
to find work and contribute to Canadian society. His path
in Canada included three phases: twenty active years in the
cosmopolitan and vibrant context of Montreal, ten years
in a remote Inuit community of 400 people in the eastern
Arctic, and his latter years in the East Coast university town

of Antigonish. Antigonish has a history, primarily through the Coady Institute at St. Francis Xavier University, of international and social justice philosophy and education. Joanne had the academic qualifications to earn the primary income. Ed got to spend what turned out to be all too little time with their two young children. And he was there to help the whole community resist wars and injustice.

The remarkable thing about Ed's career in Montreal, said Joanne, at Children's Hospital and McGill University, where he worked as a psychotherapist and lecturer supervising medical interns and residents, was that he hadn't been able to complete his engineer's training in the United States before he fled to Canada. The Vietnam War era, as with most wars, was littered with those between the ages of sixteen and twenty-five who left home and everything that they had known, owned, or started. Ed got lucky in Montreal with a learn-on-the-job program in the new field of child psychology at the hospitals:

> One of the early jobs Ed found in Canada was that of parking lot attendant at the Montreal Jewish Hospital.… Ed had a curiosity about the world and about the people in it, so in that capacity he frequently entered into conversations with the hospital personnel. Conversations in the late '60s frequently turned to politics—whether it was the Vietnam war, Quebec sovereignty, or Canada's role in defining its core values as different from those of its giant neighbour to the South. Many of the hospital

professionals that Ed interacted with were impressed by his intelligence, sharp political analysis, and strong convictions to work for social and economic and political justice. The 1960s in Canada and Quebec were a time for political and social reimagination. Some of the best jewels of Canadian social thought were emerging as structures and organizations....Ed just happened to be at the right time at the right place, to become involved in an initiative that would chart the course of his professional career.

In the 1960s the field of child psychiatry was a very emerging discipline. Adult psychiatry was well established. The psychological understandings of children's development and practices and therapies to support them were not really on the landscape in Canada. An innovative program was being launched at the Montreal Jewish General hospital where interns from various backgrounds were being accepted into a program to train as psychotherapists to work with children and their families....Several key leaders in the program came to know Ed and felt he would be a very desirable candidate for the program. Ed applied, was admitted, and underwent a robust training program. He became particularly interested in behavioural analysis and a family systems approach to working with children. He spent his professional career in Montreal working in clinics at the Jewish General Hospital, at Weredale House, formerly called the Boys Home of Montreal, the Montreal Children's Hospital, and as a lecturer at McGill University.

Ed had a profound respect for children and their ability to make sense of their world, in their own way. It is this single quality for which he gained the impressive reputation that he had among the Montreal and Quebec psychotherapy and educational community. Ed felt that children and youth were often patronized and poorly understood. Ed also had the gift of being able to provide the adults in a child's life, be they parents or guardians, educators or health professionals, with the fundamental understanding that children's behaviour was purposeful and was a means of communication. When behaviour was understood in this manner, Ed was able to help care providers find ways to teach appropriate social skills to replace behaviour that was undesirable, ineffective and/ or potentially damaging. Ed was frequently called upon to give presentations to schools and agencies working with children....It would be his reputation as an expert in child and youth behaviour that would later take Ed to Nunavut.

Nunavut is where Ed met Joanne. They became colleagues and then a couple, and the Arctic is where their children were born. Joanne was a young teacher/administrator in Nunavut. Her school board had decided that they needed community-based education, the opposite of residential schools, but it had no idea how to go about it. Joanne sought advice: "The woman that I spoke to said, 'Oh, you need to get in touch with Ed Miller at

the Montreal Children's Hospital. He can teach people
the skills in behavioural programming, and very importantly he believes in the model you are using. He's not a
fan of special classes for kids with behaviour problems.
He's your man."

Continued involvement in social justice issues was a
hallmark of Ed's life, as it was of the lives of many of the
Vietnam War resister generation. Ed's commitment to
activism certainly characterized his Canadian life, from
Montreal, to Nunavut, and finally to Antigonish. Here is
an email notice of an anti-war protest that Ed organized
in the year of his death:

From: "Ed Miller"
Subject: Peter MacKay Declares War, Antigonish Says
No to Warmonger!
Date: Tue, 11 Mar 2003

Peter MacKay, the federal Member of Parliament for
Pictou-Antigonish-Guysborough declared today that he
wants Canada to go to war against the people of Iraq. In
a statement made on a tour of Western Canada he said
that Canada should join in war on Iraq with or without
support from the United Nations and with or without
European allies.

MacKay said that Canada would lose its credibility
in the US unless it joined in war on Iraq. Let's tell Peter
MacKay what we think of his warmongering!

Wednesday, 8:30–9:30 a.m. and 11:30–12:30 p.m.
Kirk Building, 219 Main Street Antigonish (at
    Church St.)

Come out to visit MacKay's office and bring your
signs, leaflets, statements, ideas and songs while we wait!

In his involvement in this anti-war protest at McKay's
office we can see that Ed clearly felt called to action, and this
ongoing social activism was not uncommon among Vietnam
War resisters, as John Hagan notes in *Northern Passage*:

> The politically active resisters…became part of a variety
> of social networks that produced patterns of commit-
> ment that have persisted to the present.…
>
> Some Americans who came limited their resistance
> to the act of migration in response to draft and mili-
> tary laws. The majority of the Toronto resisters in my
> sample, however, actively protested the war before leav-
> ing the United States and continued their active protest
> after arriving in Canada. The persistence to this day of
> political activism in the lives of these American resisters
> is a measure of the directedness of their migration and
> the life-determining impact of their decision to come
> to Canada.[13]

Ed had read *Northern Passage*, and Joanne says Ed felt
that Hagan had "got the story right."

Ed Miller's legacy to Joanne and the children is clear. Others in Antigonish and the Atlantic region have strong memories of his leadership as well. As Joanne recalls,

Sister Marion Sheridan, an activist from the Sisters of Saint Martha's who worked alongside Ed in the Antigonish Coalition for Economic Justice (1997–2003), remembers Ed's comments. "We were working on an affordable housing project. Ed reminded us that having understanding of the oppression theory is important for those of us doing anti-poverty work, but we must be humble and aware that the voices of those who have experienced class oppression must be laid alongside, not subordinate to, class theory. Having lived in the projects he had deep insider knowledge in a way that many of the rest of us did not. He was a big believer in listening to the people closest to the experience."[14]

Joanne also recounts another time Ed organized their community:

In 1989 the Parliament of Canada passed a unanimous resolution to eradicate child poverty by the year 2000. In 1995 the UN declared October 17 as International Day for the Eradication of Poverty, naming economic injustice and the wealth gap as a leading source of other inequities. Yet, while the rhetoric to eradicate poverty was high, ideologies of neo-liberalism and forces such as the globalization of capital were increasing, rather than reducing, the wealth gap nationally and internationally. Ed decided to join with others in Antigonish....

Ed, along with members of the Antigonish Women's Resource Centre, was a key founder [of] the Antigonish Coalition for Economic Justice (ACEJ), which brought together various single-interest groups to shine a spotlight on poverty and its root causes. Members from the local women's centre, various religious communities, the Catholic organization Development and Peace, several local unions, interested university faculty, and community members all came together.

Joanne notes that Ed had a variety of skills as an activist, and these were recognized early and used continually throughout his life:

Ed was a confident and articulate public speaker. And he loved organizing and had an ability to be imaginative in his organizing but also paid meticulous attention to detail. Ed's leadership was recognized, and he grew to be a very active member of the anti-war movement in Brooklyn. He had a particular love and skill for making leaflets and saw the power in the leaflet to change ideas. He learned the skills of silk screen printing and was an early adopter of the personal computer, particular Macintosh computers, for their impressive desktop publishing features, including interesting fonts and graphics.[15]

Ed's talent for graphic arts was nowhere more evident than in the 2000 World March for Women. Antigonish had its own marches for thirty-three weeks using variations of his logos.

And the Antigonish Women's Resource Centre remembers 2000–01 as one of its proud moments. It helped to organize, with Ed's talent for protest, weekly World March of Women events from March 8, International Women's Day, to October 17, International Day for the Eradication of Poverty.

The Iraq War was the lingering/festering concern of Vietnam War resisters. We have seen this concern in Dennis Bartels and will see it again in the sections on Dr. Michael Klein and Steven Bush. In the 2000s, Ed put his graphics to work on that American war. In the Iraq War era, Canada treated resisters who fled to Canadian soil so differently from how it treated Vietnam War resisters in the late 1960s.

While Joanne continues to be inspired by Ed's legacy, her mature work related to activism in education had already started when she met Ed in the Arctic, and it continues in her work today. St. Francis Xavier University education students under her direction have an interactive experience with the Truth and Reconciliation Commission. Joanne and the students are attuned to the needs of the most marginalized groups:

Our BEd students were able to hear firsthand from Mi'kmaw students the intergenerational trauma that was caused by the residential school experience. And most importantly they see that it is part of their job as teachers in Canada to teach the truth about our colonial history that includes cultural genocide so that, as Senator Sinclair said, "we can get back to the friendship" that was intended to be between Mi'kmaw and non-Mi'kmaw peoples.[16]

After Joanne and Ed started their family, Ed was the primary parent, and he actively passed on his social consciousness and taught his children, Marion and Carl, about injustices in the world. Joanne has many memories of the children's involvement:

One activity that both children really enjoyed was the cruise missile project. In 2003 there was grave concern that Canada would join in the war against Iraq, which we now know was based on the false claims of destroying "weapons of mass destruction."...Ed and several other activists had the idea that a model of a cruise missile could be built out of papier maché and used to lead a march down Main Street. Inside the cruise missile there would be school supplies and toys and health supplies. The march would end with a rally, and at the rally Ed would talk about the dollars involved in building a cruise missile ($20 million in 2003). The financial and human cost of this destructive weapon would be highlighted. In an attempt to show how swords can be

turned into ploughshares, the missiles would be broken apart at the end of the rally by children, and the
health and education materials that could enhance
people's lives could be demonstrated. Marion and Carl
immensely enjoyed the whole experience of building
the cruise missile.

For the family, Ed is still a guide to be cherished, lis-
tened to, and lived with each day. Joanne explains that

cancer turned out to be a fight Ed would not win. In
the summer of 2002, while in Montreal, Ed had several
severe pains that took him to the emergency room. After
an operation to remove the pancreatic cancer in Halifax,
Ed wanted to be sure that he explored every avenue, and
he made a trip to Montreal to get advice from some of
his colleagues in the medical community there.

Ed came back with crushing news. When he directly
asked the surgeon, "Will I live to see my son's bar
mitzvah?" (which would have been in 2009), the surgeon told him "You may not make it till summer." Ed
described cancer as the only fight he fought that was
not ideological. Cancer simply *was*. During the winter of
2003, Ed recovered from surgery and actually felt quite
"well." The events of the world do not stand still for any
of us, and war in Iraq was becoming increasingly possible. Ed took up his activist stance. It was during this
period that he worked on the cruise missile project. Ed's

wish was to remain at home with the family in a context that could be "normal."

With the support of an excellent palliative care team, family, friends, and colleagues from StFX, arrangements were made for Ed to be at home. Ed was able to slip away on July 21, 2003, in the early morning in his bed. I woke Carl, seven at the time, and Marion, eleven, and all three of us lay with Ed on the bed. Through tears, I explained that maybe this was the time to "let Daddy go" so he could leave the pain behind.

Ed struggled with who his community really was. He had been forced to leave his New York community as a war resister at eighteen and come to Canada. He left his Montreal community to join me in the Arctic at forty. At almost fifty, he picked up again and began a new life in Antigonish.

Ed was buried in the graveyard in East Margaree, the small Cape Breton community from which both my parents had come. In Montreal two memorial services were held. In Halifax Larry and Judy Haiven organized a memorial of Halifax activists.

The Haivens, noted activists in their own right, told me in 2016 that, though they had met Ed near the end of his life, he had made a huge impression on them. His life should be honoured. Ed, they summed up, was extremely intelligent and wise, a gifted international strategist operating on a very small stage.

Joanne sees Ed's legacy in every aspect of the family's life:

> The obvious and in many ways deepest was becoming my life partner as we created our family together. Ed influenced my professional practice as an educator by his orientation towards children and his deep understanding of children's behaviour. And he was simply one of the smartest people and the most well-rounded person I have ever met.
>
> Most of all I see Ed in our children. As Leon Dubinsky, Cape Breton Jewish songwriter, says, "We rise again in the faces of our children."

The children of Ed and Joanne, now young adults—Carl, twenty-one, and Marion, twenty-five—have also found ways to make their world a better place. A proud mother, Joanne summarizes their achievements:

> Since graduating high school, Marion has been based in Montreal for her studies, where she is involved in anti-capitalist, feminist, and queer organizing....She was active in the 2012 student strike, the "Maple Spring," taking part in the *chorale de la grève* ("strikers' choir").
>
> Carl Aaron Jimmy Iqtuaq Miller is now studying in physics and engineering at St. Francis Xavier University. Carl talks about his lessons from Ed. "What I learned from Ed Miller as a father was that nearly every person

you meet has an opinion on a subject that is very much worth hearing….When I would come along to run errands with him during his day, I have so many memories of him having very deep and interesting conversations with people from all aspects of life in my small town….And when I compare the movement and life of New York to the quiet of a 4,000-person town, it makes me realize that, if you take the time to look, you can be interested anywhere. He taught me to stay curious about not only the world but the people that fill it."

The family continues with dedication to, and passion for, Ed's legacy of peacemaking, undertaking war protests, and creating spaces for the marginalized in Canada. His life's work as an "American refugee" has become their lives' work too.

BONNIE SHERR KLEIN AND MICHAEL KLEIN: THE BEST DECISION WE EVER MADE

The Klein grandparents, Michael's parents, always expected "the knock on the door." The knock might come from anti-union forces, anti-socialist and anti-communist factions, or police supporting the Cold War. So the next generation, Michael Klein, who later married Bonnie Sherr, could hear echoes of the knock in their minds and memories too. And then the grandchildren grew up with the social justice narrative as part of their narrative.

There was always the sense in the American household of the Klein grandparents that—if you were too progressive, too much on the side of labour, civil rights, peace, education, and medical care for all, too vocal about being in solidarity with racial and other minorities—the might of the state could decide to silence you. And suddenly. The anticipated knocks on the door were not in the Soviet Union or South America; they were in the United States.

Michael's father, animator Phil Klein, went on the picket lines and then was let go from the Disney Corporation during the strike of 1941. This strike has been called the "Civil War of Animation." The Kleins had to decide whether to be on the side of worker slaves and their capitalistic bosses or on the side of the free.[17]

To the outside eye, The Walt Disney Studio seemed a magical place where the finest animated cartoons in the world [were] made. Mickey Mouse, Donald Duck and Goofy were loved by everyone from Shirley Temple to Mussolini. Walt Disney's first feature length cartoon, *Snow White and the Seven Dwarfs*, earned four times more than any movie in 1938. It won a special Oscar and famed Russian filmmaker Sergei Eisenstein called it the greatest motion picture ever made.

Behind the PR, the Walt Disney Studio had grown from a few friends in a storefront to an industrial plant where 1,293 employees labored six days a week. Disney plowed the profits back into new studio facilities and bolder experiments in animation and stereophonic sound. But wages remained low across the board and bonuses or raises were given irregularly at the whim of management. No screen credit was allowed other than Walt's. The next films *Pinocchio* and *Fantasia* failed to generate the same success as *Snow White*.

Be it mid-life disillusion, the death of his mother or the impending World War that was drying up overseas box office,…by 1941, Uncle Walt the folksy cartoonist became Mr. Disney, the worry-racked capitalist. Walt may still have thought of himself as just one of the guys, but to many he was the boss. He grew isolated.…Then he could be seen walking around the empty tables looking to see what they were doing.[18]

The next generation of Kleins had a decision to make, too. The first moment of truth for Michael and Bonnie was the Vietnam War. Bonnie recalled that pivotal time in their lives in an opinion piece she wrote for *The Tyee* in 2013, shortly after being appointed to the Order of Canada:

September 1967. We are holding our breath. We have to get into Canada immediately or Michael, my new husband, will be jailed. At the advice of the Montreal Committee to Aid War Resisters, we have arrived at Dorval Airport after midnight, when mostly sympathetic French-Canadian immigration officers are on duty. Michael has a hastily-offered letter of employment from Montreal Children's Hospital. Twenty minutes later, we are relieved to be welcomed as landed immigrants! We are among the wave of over 200,000 Vietnam-era women and men who became an integral part of the Canadian mosaic.

Before our immigration, Michael had been offered a position as a medical officer in the American military but had planned to go to jail rather than serve the Vietnam War in any capacity. Serendipitously, the day he received the commission, I was at a seminar for documentary filmmakers and had just seen the Canadian documentary *Mills of the Gods*. In it, director Beryl Fox bravely sat filming from the cockpit of a helicopter as it sprayed napalm on a Vietnamese village. We Americans who opposed the war knew about the atrocities, but our U.S. media never exposed them. A Canadian woman did, and the Canadian Broadcasting Corporation aired her film.[19]

Michael and Bonnie entered the Canada with which most of the Vietnam War resisters fell in love: peace loving, welcoming to those resisting war, courageous enough to differ strongly from the powerful United States, offering universal health care, funding fearless cultural institutions. What was not to like?

Later they realized that Canada had rolled out the welcome mat to well-educated immigrants, reversing the brain drain; to war resisters who were almost

100 percent white, not of colour; and to those with the resources and connections to immigrate suddenly and find almost instant employment. Later they also realized that Canada was participating in the Vietnam War, just not on the ground.[20]

These more nuanced understandings did not occur until the new millennium. The amazing place where the Kleins became landed immigrants in twenty minutes was Quebec in the late 1960s. And life for them evolved with meaningful work, bilingualism, and a healthy young family. Michael, as promised, found a position at the Montreal Children's Hospital, and Bonnie found her way into the National Film Board for the first of two golden eras in which she had central roles.

Challenge for Change, a program directed by the icon of activist documentary filmmakers, George Stoney, existed at the NFB from 1968 to 1980. This was definitely gold for Bonnie. Stoney was one of her professional idols, and she got to work on this community-based program that both documented and catalyzed change.

During this period, Bonnie worked on a series about community organizer Saul Alinsky. All of the episodes were interesting and radical and featured the voices of the marginalized. I will focus on one episode about Rochester, New York. As you will see, it soon hits close to home.

Until 1964, Rochester thought of itself—and perhaps the rest of the United States thought of Rochester—as the perfect northern liberal town. It was a haven from the brutality of the racist south and the industrial north. Rochester was a kinder, gentler place. Eastman Kodak was the biggest employer, and what could be a more humane business than providing people with equipment to take lovely family photos?

Then race riots erupted for three days in 1964 in Rochester, telling the world that there was something wrong with the picture of this small city. Alinsky came to organize. Challenge for Change was there and chronicled the stories that ripped the peaceful, non-racist face off Rochester. The black community demanded 600 jobs from Kodak. These jobs, the community stated, should include chemists who were black and university-educated in the north, and not just janitors.[21]

Three years after moving to Canada, the Klein family faced a difficult decision. Now free to travel back to the United States, Michael having been declared "unfit" for military service by his draft board, they wanted to return there for medical training not available in Canada. However, that training was to be in Rochester, the small city that Bonnie knew all too well from her time with the Challenge for Change program. This was the Rochester in denial about racist practices in employment, housing, and what a decent education bought a black person, even in the liberal north. Nonetheless, the Kleins decided to return and for a short time made Rochester their home. Bonnie started a community television initiative in Rochester, and Michael received his additional medical training.

Then they returned to Canada in 1975, a second immigration. Studio D, the still unequalled women's studio of the NFB, opened up for Bonnie. Medicare began for Michael and the entire Canadian population. These were terrific times to be Canadians with their skill sets, as Bonnie explains:

> After five years in the U.S., we chose to immigrate to Canada a second time. In the interval, Canada had initiated universal Medicare. The NFB had created Studio D, the first and only government-sponsored feminist filmmaking unit in the world. Most important to us, Canada had the values and spirit, different from those in the U.S., in which we wanted to raise our children. As far as we knew, Canada had stayed out of wars and coups in foreign countries; it chose to be a peace-maker. We were not naive about this "kinder and gentler place": Canada had its share of violence, racism and sexism, but [it] also had the motivation and institutions to address its problems. Here we have remained and thrived, Canadian citizens by choice, the best choice we ever made.[22]

Honours in medicine, which have followed Michael throughout his career, have come from working with and advocating for the marginalized, in this case women, including women in rural communities. In 2017, Michael was recognized for his work by being appointed a Member of the Order of Canada. The citation reads as follows:

Michael Klein has played a vital role in placing maternity care at the heart of family medicine. Refusing to serve in the United States medical corps during the Vietnam War, he fled to Canada in 1967 and went on to become a family practitioner, a pediatrician and a professor at McGill University and the University of British Columbia. Concerned by the harmful effects of certain medical interventions during the birth process, he advocated for family-friendly birth practices, including the re-introduction of midwifery, the promotion of doulas and the elimination of routine intrusive interventions such as episiotomy—all of which are now widely accepted in birth settings.[23]

Bonnie Sherr Klein's most famous contribution to Studio D is *Not a Love Story: A Film about Pornography*. The Toronto International Film Festival selected it as one of Canada's Top 10 Showcase in 2015. The NFB's original 1982 study guide outlined the cultural significance of Studio D and of this particular film:

Not a Love Story was produced by Studio D of the NFB's English Production branch. Founded in 1974, the studio is presently the only publicly funded women's film unit in the world. Although the studio includes male filmmakers as well, its main objective remains to bring a woman's perspective to social issues and to act as a catalyst for social change through the medium of film.

Not a Love Story represents a significant contribution to the work that the studio has done. Many of the films made by the studio explore the position of women in society and the attitudes and relationships that exist between women and men. Pornography, because it perpetuates fantasies that both create and respond to cultural stereotypes, is an important and revealing aspect of this study.[24]

Dr. Michael Klein, Invested as a Member of the Order of Canada, 2017 (Photo by Sergeant Johanie Maheu)

Not to be overlooked among the Kleins' contributions to Canada are their children, who returned from the United States to Canada with their parents in 1975, never to leave. With good reason, Michael and Bonnie are very proud of their children.

Seth Klein is the founding director of the Canadian Centre for Policy Alternatives in British Columbia. His research deals primarily with welfare policy, poverty, inequality, and economic security. A social activist for over thirty years and a former teacher, Seth holds degrees in education, international relations, and political science. He is a co-chair of the BC Poverty Reduction Coalition, an advisory board member for the Columbia Institute's Centre for Civic Governance, and an adviser and instructor for Next Up, a leadership program for young people committed to social and environmental justice.

Naomi Klein is an award-winning journalist, syndicated columnist, and author of the international bestsellers *This Changes Everything: Capitalism vs the Climate* (2014), *The Shock Doctrine: The Rise of Disaster Capitalism* (2007), and *No Logo: Taking Aim at the Brand Bullies* (2000). *This Changes Everything* was an instant *New York Times* bestseller and is being translated into over twenty-five languages. Nominated for multiple awards, it won the 2014 Hilary Weston Writers' Trust Prize for Non-Fiction. Her first book, *No Logo*, was also an international bestseller.[25]

Seth and Naomi, the third Klein generation, make people aware of the abuses of power, the troubles of working people, and how much Canadians must continue to stand on guard.

Bonnie's next big round of activism after Studio D came about because of a life-changing illness. A major stroke in 1987 almost killed Bonnie. In her first film after the stroke, *Shameless: The Art of Disability* (2006), she quips that, if you're going to have a life-threatening illness, it helps to be married to a physician. It must also have been life changing for the two teenage children, who suddenly found themselves responsible for someone else. Bonnie slowly made the transition to a disability rights activist. For the Klein family, there was a phase in which all four had to work on the same project: that of bringing Bonnie back into the land of the living and the world of creative possibility.

Bonnie is a founder of Kickstart (formerly the Society for Disability Arts and Culture), whose mission is to produce and present works by artists with disabilities and to promote artistic excellence among these artists working in a variety of disciplines. Kickstart carries out this mission by producing cross-disciplinary festivals of disability arts and culture guided by these key objectives:

- to encourage and support artists to create and present authentic interpretations of the disability experience,
- to provide opportunities for the development and advancement of artists with disabilities, and
- to promote practices that will make the arts more accessible to all members of the Canadian public.[26]

Bonnie Sherr Klein, 2013 (Photo by dm gillis)

For many in the Vietnam War resister immigrant community, Canada was gold at the time. However, in the new millennium, as they live out their senior years, these resisters are not fooled. They have been in the forefront, calling Canada to account about the Iraq War and how differently resisters/dodgers/deserters of that war have been treated. Canada did not welcome them and in fact has been deporting them. Michael told me that I couldn't talk about their Vietnam War resister generation without talking about the Iraq War resisters. He and other 1960s immigrants—such as well-known retired CBC Radio host Andy Barrie—have made their voices heard and have unsettled a comfortable Canada regarding its treatment of resisters to the more recent war.[27] These immigrants aren't saying "I got to the Promised Land, now close the border!" They were activists upon arrival. They still are. And they believe strongly that it is their duty to voice concerns about Canada and some of its present policies, as Bonnie did in her 2013 opinion piece in *The Tyee*:

> [Canada is] following in the footsteps of the U.S. into countries in which we have no business. We loudly support Israel's occupation [of] and expansion into Palestinian territories. Our country is closing its doors to immigrants and refugees, including political refugees, except those who can invest large sums in our economy or contribute cheap labour as temporary foreign workers.
>
> We are compromising our historic public support for the arts and communication by starving and threatening our cultural institutions with cutbacks and commercialization. We have allowed our treasured Medicare system to atrophy rather than improve and fund it appropriately; this has made private medical care look much more attractive than it is.[28]

I asked Bonnie and Michael that question that interviewers always ask: "What are you going to do now?" Michael's reaction was, "Enough already; we're going to enjoy our grandchildren!" And that does appear to be what they are doing—except for their disability rights activism; except for their calling Canada to account for its cowardice vis-à-vis the United States; except for Michael's continuing research on maternal health; and except for their vocal support of Iraq War resisters.

For Vietnam War resisters, Canada was and is, without a doubt, a better country than the United States. However, when we Canadians can admit our participation in that war, acknowledge that the original welcome of these resisters depended on a context of racial and demographic discrimination, and accept that we have adopted a very different stance toward Iraq War resisters more recently, then Canada will move toward being a much better country.

STEVEN BUSH AND FRANK CANINO:
ACT YOUR WAY NORTH

An artists' cooperative apartment building, with a splendid, well-equipped performance space and an art gallery, is our Toronto residence. On a beautiful, sunny, Sunday afternoon in October 2016, an audience gathers to hear an early reading of a new script about US expatriates living in Canada. The playwright is Frank Canino. And two of the immigrant actors on stage, who have US

expat experience, armed with scripts on music stands, are
Catherine Marrion and Steven Bush.

Playwright Frank and actor Steven have known each
other since forever, it seems. In 1961, Frank was an actor/
stage manager and Steven an actor in the same company
in Cincinnati. Then they followed very different paths to
Canada, but their paths crossed again in Canadian theatre.
Frank took a somewhat accidental path in his avoidance
of the Vietnam War, in which he had intended to fight,
and his Canadian journey began in Nova Scotia. Steven
was a much more committed draft resister and began his
Canadian odyssey in Toronto. Yet both can be seen in the
present era to highlight similar issues in their art.

Catherine, an expressive arts therapist and educator,
crossed the international border in the 1960s, settling in
British Columbia, another of Canada's large Vietnam War
resister and left-leaning locations. She became a friend and
theatre colleague of Steven in the 1980s. On their twentieth
anniversary of being together, in 2017, they got married.

The need for consistent moral—almost religious—
authenticity radiates from Steven Bush the person and the
artist, born in 1944 in Washington, DC. He always seems
to test his work, his statements, his stances, his use of personal energy with being the same person publicly and pri-
vately, professionally and personally.

Although from a distance, I have known Steven for
years and admired his skill, honesty, and detail as an actor,
I didn't know much about his draft resister story until

doing research for this book. We talked over a delicious lunch in the large, open-concept apartment that he shares with Catherine in Toronto's Parkdale district.

Steven does not disavow his early formation from his mother's side as a Jehovah's Witness. There is a religious consistency there. Nor does he disavow his early formation in Mississippi, where his father was much less conservative than many in the community.[29] There was a belief there that change for the better can happen.

Steven's career in theatre was building when the Vietnam War began. He was turned down for conscientious objector status in the mid-1960s. Then, during his medical assessment for the draft it was discovered that Steven had a heart murmur, and he was given a medical deferment as a result. He sent his draft card to peace activists to return to the Selective Service System during a massive peace rally at the Pentagon. The FBI paid a visit to his home. He was certain that they would return.

In 1969, Steven decided to take a trip to Canada to "clear his head." He found accommodation in Toronto's draft resister central housing at 218 and 224 McCaul Street. He lived there while continuing his career as an actor. By the early 1970s, Steven was deeply invested in Canada. Not wanting to keep "straddling the border," he became a Canadian citizen in 1975.[30]

His Canadian life has had many personal and career benefits. First, Steven had that rare good fortune: almost consistent employment in the theatre. It is possible for me to look at that and say, "Of course, he's a tall white guy." However, he has also been employed almost continually in the type of social activist theatre that he believes is essential. It is a wonderful gift to do the arts work that one thinks is important, and Steven has been fortunate to be in the right places at the right times to do that work. Second, he has been teaching at the University of Toronto, while Catherine has been teaching at Humber College, so they have had the consistent income that postsecondary education generates to create a comfortable life. Third, Canada's universal health care paid for thousands of dollars of orthopedic work that Steven needed with increasing age and some congenital difficulties. All of these are reasons for him to be fond of Canada, but there remain issues here that need to be addressed through the arts and protests.

Steven is still an activist because of a number of troublesome realities in the contemporary world. Close to home is the high cost and gentrification of his neighbourhood. Both Steven and his adult son were supportive of the Parkdale Rent Strike 2017. The group attained some hard-won victories. Tenants withheld rent because of alleged shoddy and unclean conditions, combined with rent hikes that they maintained were being used to push out lower-income tenants. The tenants won. Repairs have been promised and rent increases halted.[31]

Steven's one-man show *Beating the Bushes* threads through his expatriate history from Vietnam War resistance to the present, employing poetic reverie, family memoir, stand-up comedy, and brief dialogues. In one of the scenes, George Bush Senior (who may be Steven's distant cousin) receives an honorary doctorate at convocation at the University of Toronto:

Steven Bush Character: University of Toronto… venerable institution for which I happily work… November 1997.…

"Bush off Campus!"

Now I don't take this personally.…I've gotten beyond that!…But I am beginning to wonder why…*why* did I exit Richard Nixon's Amerika lo so many years ago? To live in a country where George Bush, Sr.—Dubya's Dad—a man arguably worse than even Richard Nixon—is given an Honourary bloody Degree?!!!

1968. The Vietnam War (according to Americans): The American War (according to Vietnamese). Lots, *lots* of people dying—thousands of my countrymen, many thousand more Vietnamese.

Some things stick in the mind forever—like the first photo you ever see of what the human body looks like after it's been hit by napalm.…

Protests grow as the carnage grows. Two public figures best situated to lead mass democratic opposition… Martin Luther King, Jr. and Bobby Kennedy…are felled, so the story goes, by lone assassins. But we no longer believe in "lone assassins" and the "police riot" in the streets of Chicago, the attacks on Black activists, the unbelievable election of warmonger Nixon.…These are lifting the scales from our eyes, they are forcing us to see what martyred Brother Malcolm X saw when he called the American Dream "the American Nightmare."

And so even not-especially-brave people like me are getting arrested at peace demos.

In Atlanta the FBI shows up on my porch. Why? Along with thousands of other young American males, I'd turned in my military draft card to a massive rally at the Pentagon. This makes me arrestable.

Sooo: To go underground? Go to jail? *Or*…go to another country? Canada suddenly becomes very attractive.

February '69: Arrive Toronto cold bright day with snow on the ground. 1st glimpse of the U of T: Looks like a university should—just like a *movie* university!

I stay. And the longer I stay the more attractive Canada becomes. I start to realize life is better here. Universal health care: "A poor person can actually afford to get sick in Canada."

The NDP? What? A Socialist party? You've got to be kidding! With lots of members? *Whaat*??? Holding seats…in Parliament???!!!

All this *and* a Prime Minister who has publicly declared that "Canada should be a refuge from militarism."

Indeed the odds of being *shot*—by civilians or the government—do seem noticeably lower here.

1975: I take an oath to Her Majesty.

The judge presiding speaks about the "absurdity" of Canada—how in terms of historical logic, Canada shouldn't exist…and yet it does.

I cannot tell you how much this appeals to me.

I mean, can you imagine an *American* judge… addressing a group of soon-to-be-Americans…about the absurdity of the *United States*?…

Since I took the Oath, this beloved country has sustained a lot of damage: By the late 1990's—after NAFTA—the line between Canada and the United States has grown thinner.

November 19th 1997: On the beautiful Hart House stage, Canada's premier university bestows an Honourary Degree on George Herbert Walker Bush.

However, across the road, on this seriously freezing day—a couple thousand teachers and students have something to say about this bloody *dis*-honourable degree:

"DRUG DEALER…WAR CRIMINAL…CIA SPY"

Is this what universities are supposed to do?

Give out awards to war criminals?

"BUSH OFF CAMPUS!!!"[32]

Beating the Bushes is a biting hybrid of a political science book, historical analysis, a theatrical show, and an op-ed piece. What is wrong with the contemporary Canadian picture? After all, it has most of what we like to tell ourselves about the Canada-US story: the Vietnam War resisters were welcomed to Canada; they stayed, contributed, and prospered. They are good citizens, exercising their right to peaceful protest.

What is wrong with this picture is that the honorary doctorate for Bush symbolically reduces Canadian sovereignty. And, much more importantly, for the past ten years, the War Resisters Support Campaign, in which

Steven is an active participant, hasn't been able to per-suade Canada that the Iraq War resisters deserve a wel-come. These resisters are different: they are women and men, and some are working class or downright poor, not so well educated, and visible and audible minorities. They do not move seamlessly into universities, the civil service, publishing, and the arts. In fact, some of them are more like refugees, and Canada might have to provide them with some initial education and job training. Perhaps most importantly, in the new millennium, Canada does not feel quite so independent from the United States as it did during the Vietnam War era.

Organizers of the War Resisters Support Campaign wrote to Steven in 2017 that "the campaign is holding steady and continuing to push for status for all the resist-ers, but it is slow going and the number of campaign-ers has shrunk substantially so it is a challenge for sure." Steven commented to me: "I guess what we have here is an instance of Canada *failing* American refugees. (And the country has had over ten years *not* to fail them.)" In the same email, he offered this quip on Canada-US rela-tions and the Iraq War resisters: "You would have thought it would have been a 'no-brainer' for the Trudeau gov-ernment to have granted safe haven to this crop of resist-ers—i.e., as a way to distance itself further from the Harper Gang with little or no cost to itself—but apparently not."[33]

The Vietnam War resisters profiled in this book are united in speaking about the Iraq War resisters. They desperately want Canada to be the better country to which they fled, which means welcoming and being a refuge for new arrivals. It is one of their most passionate current causes.

Playwright Steven Bush (Photo by Nir Bareket)

Playwright Frank Canino takes up the contemporary cry of war resisters in fiction. His new script is "Two Holidays," the theme of which, he says, is "the outsider." It bills itself as a "serious comedy," and that is accurate. The script is framed by some deeply disturbing problems and some laughter-inducing solutions. A group of US expatriates resident in Canada gather, just across the border from upstate New York, to "celebrate" on American Thanksgiving. The fictional dinner takes place as the results of the first Obama election are coming in on radio and television. The characters are of the Vietnam War resister generation, which means that they are in their late sixties to late seventies. In short, they are getting old. One man missing from the annual dinner is a casualty of alcohol and mental health issues. A second is attempting to take his own life during the dinner (without success), in part because of guilt that he hasn't maintained his political ideals.

JUDY

You can't commit suicide on Thanksgiving.

DAN

This is Canada. Yankee Thanksgiving doesn't count here.

PATTY

Sweetheart, let's talk. We know it's a bad time for you.

DAN

It's not just me. Stupid bastards just put Bush in for a second term. Once is bad; twice is ridiculous.

PATTY

We don't live down there anymore. Bush is their
problem.

DAN

It's worse here. Friggin' Conservatives takin'
over Parliament. We're properly fucked.

JUDY

At least we don't have Nixon and Kissinger.

PATTY

Sweetie, it has to be something worse than politics.

DAN

Yes! I got kicked out of the YCL [Young
Communists League].

PATTY

The YCL got dissolved last year.

DAN

Right! So I can't ever get back in.[34]

Frank Canino was born in 1938 in Chicago and raised
there, but he has spent most of his adult working life
in Canada. His writing projects range from film scripts
to musicals and dramas. After his thoroughly Roman

Catholic elementary, secondary, and university education (Loyola University 1952–56), he studied theatre in Washington, DC. There he met a priest who said, "You must go to Canada." Not listening to that advice immediately, in 1962 Frank took a part-time teaching job in the Bronx. He hated it.

Playwright Frank Canino (Courtesy of Frank Canino)

Then in 1963 an ad for a miracle job appeared: a teacher of drama was wanted at Saint Francis Xavier University in Antigonish, Nova Scotia. Frank was uniquely qualified for this small Canadian university with an international conscience. His entire education had been in Catholic institutions. He was a professional theatre person. And he had an urgent desire to get out of the Bronx. Frank didn't intend to stay long. Moving from New York City to Antigonish was a big culture shock for him. But then his students won prizes at the Dominion Drama Festival. For *The Wakefield Cycle*, Frank got the Best Director award and they all got the Best Production award. StFX wanted Frank to stay. He was a hit as a drama teacher.

In 1966–67, the famous centennial era again, Frank was awarded a Canada Council grant to tour Canadian theatres. It was all very exciting, and he met important figures such as Leon Major, the founding artistic director of Halifax's Neptune Theatre and the director general of Toronto Arts Productions.

Soon Frank began to look at the United States with dismay, especially after the riots in Washington, DC, in 1968. Black rage erupted all over the United States in the aftermath of Martin Luther King Jr.'s murder. Anger was felt deeply in the capital, where emancipated slaves had tried to find shelter since the time of Lincoln. The rage boiled over because of historical and ongoing unequal employment rates, segregated housing in the worst communities, police officers who targeted blacks, and an education system that ignored black children. Meanwhile, said Frank, his own family was "becoming more right wing."

In 1969, he got a teaching job at the University of Ottawa. His draft board, with whom he had remained in communication, declared him unfit to serve in the war: he was very short, homosexual (perhaps that was a problem?), and had some misgivings about the United States on the international scene. However, Frank said that he would have served if the US Army had accepted him. He had intended to join the Vietnam War when requested to do so.

In 1972–73, Frank was in Europe and there he had the opportunity to look at the United States from a global perspective, from the view of Peter Brook's International Theatre Company. His political eyes were opened by this company. The multinational assembly of actors, dancers, musicians, and other performers travelled widely in the Middle East and Africa in the early 1970s. They were on a three-year "pilgrimage" to answer the question "What are the common stories, the recognizable shorthands, the instant abstractions, the shared outlines of story and character with which an international group could work?"[35] The varying world perspectives that Frank gained in 1972 convinced him not to go back to the United States. He became a Canadian citizen and obtained a Canadian passport. He has (almost) shed his American identity.

In the "Two Holidays" script, worry among the expats about the politics of the two countries is constant. The gourmet cook character, responsible for the American

Thanksgiving meal, drinks far too much. The men are almost "typical" Vietnam War vets fifty years later: alcohol, drugs, suicide, purposelessness. The women, however, are different. They are working vigorously against the Iraq War:

ALICE
Weren't we beautiful!?

DAVID
Only for a while, m'dear.

PATTY
O hush, Davie. It's a wonderful picture....
   [They raise their glasses.]
Here's to us: foreigners and fugitives, exiles and ex-pats ...

LORENZO
Strangers and settlers ...

JUDY
Resisters and refugees ...

DAVID
Defectors and DP's more like it ...

ALICE
But pilgrims and pioneers too! Yes?

PATTY

Yes! Thank you, America. Thank you, Canada.
Sure, we're all "from away," but we're still your
children.

DAVID

But some of us—are bastards![36]

It is the two women, an ex-nun and an ESL teacher,
who have remained most involved in political activity in
Toronto, and that is where the plot thickens. That night, in
this house near the border, they are expecting an Iraq War
resister, her husband, and their baby. Although the family
crossed into Canada without difficulty, the US authorities
would like the family returned for questioning. A police-
man stops at the house to warn the dinner party to be on
the lookout for the family. The two older women swing
into action with a plan to get the young family safely to
Toronto and the war resisters' lawyers.

The men, the old Vietnam War resisters, regret that
they haven't done enough, consistently, over time. The
women, however, are getting on with their anti-war cause
and the job of making Canada an even better place.

DAVID

It's looking good for Obama.
That's good, yes?

LORENZO

But their treatment of First Nation peoples—just as bad as in the States. Maybe worse.

DAN

And they'll tell you there's no problem with the black community. Which only means they don't lynch them.

LORENZO

So you make your choice: I skipped across the border and settled in Toronto.

DAN

Me too. Never did go back home.

BEATRIZ

Wasn't there an amnesty?

LORENZO

By that time we'd been here for a few years. We were—comfortable.

DAN

And this country—it was like a new frontier. You felt you could start all over. Unlimited opportunities.

DAVID

Only for a while.

LORENZO

You get used to a new place, and eventually you
become a different person.

PATTY

And then some of us had kids. Who would raise
their kids in the states when they could live
here?[37]

Frank didn't resist the Vietnam War draft. It resisted
him. But he already had serious questions about the
United States that was waging the war.

In 1975, he met his long-time partner and now husband, Henry, an American. They had a commuting relationship for many years, and their employment made this
possible. Thirty years later, though, in an attempt to live in
one place in their senior years, they moved to Buffalo. If
Frank has to run across the border again, it won't be far, a
stone's throw from Toronto. The 2016 presidential election
in the United States might signal that it is time to cross
that border again.

FIVE

CLOSING SNAPSHOTS
THEIR STATUS
IS "PENDING"

REFUGEES FROM HOMOPHOBIA

Las Vegas has wedding tourism. So does Hawaii. And so for a time did Canada, especially Toronto. Why? The simple answer is that Canada legalized same-gender marriages, and the rights and privileges that accompany marriage, a full ten years before the United States did.[1] I told contacts at the Metropolitan Community Church of Toronto, the largest LGBT church in North America, that I was looking for people who had changed countries as a result of the different laws in Canada, not couples who had crossed the border to get married in

Canada and then had gone back to the United States. "There was quite a lot of that," they said, smiling, "but that's not what happened to us."

Those who stayed after the champagne and dancing with friends met Canadians who had the same interests, namely religious and spiritual, and conducted long-distance commuter relationships for some time. Then jobs became available in Canada. They stayed. My sources are anonymous here because their immigration status in Canada remains pending, unsettled and uncertain.

Toronto became home for them. They got married and are on paths to living happily ever after. Frequently it meant leaving family members, networks, and connections behind and establishing new lives, just as the Vietnam War resisters did.

But by this time Canada was definitely home. The refugees from homophobia moved from a United States where they grew up, did not feel safe, and from which they now feel alienated. Canada was better for them in so many ways. As in most churches, love is talked about a lot at the Metropolitan Community Church. However, at an LGBT place of worship, the search for acceptance and safety has additional meaning. Here is an example from a sermon, "Love Makes the World Go Round":

> Our modern world…[is] dominated with ideas that drive us apart and alienate us from one another. The Book of Genesis encourages us to move toward things

because that is the only movement that creates and sustains life.

All things in the universe are part of the allurement that is God's love. Nothing exists outside of that pull.... Things happen in life, breaking it apart, but love—God's love, our love—holds it together. Everything is made out of love, held together by love, flows toward love. It's true of atoms. It's true of galaxies. And it's true of us.[2]

Canada as a politically more open place relates to the church's interpretation of faith. One of the jobs of people of faith is to tell all the "good news that you are accepted as you are." That "good news" of course includes gay, lesbian, bisexual, and transgendered souls.[3] And the refugees from homophobia seek to be citizens of and continue to make contributions to their adopted country. Their Canada includes early and nationwide equal marriage laws. And their Canada includes universal health care from which they have benefitted.

Toronto is a city that at least holds the ideal of being responsive to and responsible for all of its citizens, even if this goal breaks down in practice at times. A profound example of responsibility for all communities was the 2016 apology from Police Chief Mark Saunders for the bathhouse raids thirty-five years earlier. The Metropolitan Community Church worked with the police to make public their apology: "'The 35th anniversary of the 1981 raids is a time when the Toronto Police Service expresses its regrets for those very actions. It is also an occasion to acknowledge the lessons learned about the risks of treating any part of Toronto's many communities as not fully a part of society,' Saunders said."[4] This apology did not satisfy everyone, nor did it turn Canada into the perfect society for every member of LGBT communities. But is Canada a better society than the United States, which they'd left? The answer is a firm "Yes."

RECENT ASYLUM SEEKERS

We are once again glued to our various news sources, television screens, and electronic devices because of the number of migrants who have been crossing the Canada-US border illegally. They have come from numerous African or Middle Eastern countries, Haiti, Mexico. They would have claimed refugee status in the United States, but with Donald Trump as president that appears not to be possible. So the refugee claimants have been making their way across the border, ill-dressed, ill-fed, and housed for a time in border communities.

Our attention and our hearts are grabbed by the asylum seekers, who are often unprepared for the harsh realities of our winter weather. Cameras have been focused on the small town of Emerson, Manitoba, where migrants from Ghana, after getting lost and losing fingers and toes to frostbite as a result, crossed at a non–port of entry. Then there are the migrants who find their way to Quebec, most of them from

Haiti. The United States has said it will no longer provide shelter for Haitians who lost everything in the earthquakes.

The asylum seekers don't cross at staffed and regulated ports of entry from the United States to Canada. They cross where there are no authorities and no guidelines. They are exceptions to the rule of applying for refugee status in the first "safe" country they have entered, as Canada and the United States have referred to each other since 2002.[5] Entering Canada at an unofficial point is important because this means that the refugees will not be returned to the "safe country" of the United States (the only country that Canada considers safe in perpetuity). Obviously it is not so safe if migrants are being deported by the US to Somalia, Haiti, Syria, and other Trump-banned Muslim majority countries. Canada will not deport them while investigating their claims.

Those taking the dangerous walk apply for refugee status in Canada. The outcome of each application, of course, is uncertain. The welcome of Canada is uncertain too. It is a subject of considerable debate at this writing: if, and how, Canada, especially our largest cities, will support and house the most recent illegal border crossers. These asylum seekers have navigated the oceans and the United States to our doors. This recent wave of refugee claimants did not choose Canada; rather, the United States aggressively unchose them.[6]

The Harvard Immigration and Refugee Clinic (HIRC), which represents individuals applying for US asylum, recommends that Canada amend or rescind the safe country agreement. It is life threatening, unworkable, unsafe:

> In view of the report's findings, HIRC is urging Canada to reconsider its policy of refusing to entertain asylum claims by refugees entering Canada from the United States.…[It is] urging the Canadian government to halt enforcement of Canada's Safe Third Country Agreement with the United States. Under this Agreement…, Canada refuses to consider the claims to asylum protection of anyone entering from the United States, on the ground that the United States is a "safe country" in which to apply for asylum—a country where asylum claims will be fairly heard, and protection will be granted to legitimate refugees.[7]

We live in a period now of considerable disagreement with our best friends to the south: about trade, allies, immigration and refugee policy, safety, war, and the world's longest undefended border.

ELIZABETH (DORI) TUNSTALL: UNITED STATES SPELLS NO OPPORTUNITY

Dean Dori, as I have come to call her, proudly sporting a substantial Afro hairstyle and sipping tea, firmly states, "I would *never* get this opportunity in the United States." The opportunity? Dean of Design, with more than 125 faculty members, at the venerable, 141-year-old Ontario College of Art (and other names over the years). The opportunity at OCADU she would never get at an equivalent institution in the United States.

Dr. Elizabeth Tunstall, Dean of the Faculty of Design, OCAD University, 2016 (Photo by Martin Iskander)

Dr. Elizabeth (Dori) Tunstall is the first black dean of design at a major postsecondary school of "art and design." Dori is a great distance theoretically, aesthetically, and practically from the white gentlemen painters of the Ontario College of Art in 1876:

> OCAD University was originally established in Toronto by the Ontario Society of Artists. Back then it was called the Ontario School of Art. In 1912, it was incorporated as the Ontario College of Art, becoming the first school in Canada dedicated exclusively to the education of professional artists in fine and commercial art. In 1996, the name changed to the Ontario College of Art and Design, reflecting the growth of design programs. In 2010, to reflect the institution's status as a university granted in 2002, the school became officially known as OCAD University.[8]

Dean Dori and I have a few things in common. We began our lives in the American South; we are children of black families who owned property; we were blessed with parents who valued and believed in higher education as the most successful insurance policy; and older generations encouraged us to "Go wherever you need to go to do whatever you have to do."

We both came to Canada. It became Dori's new home in 2016. Why Canada? Why OCADU? Quickest answer: because Canadian universities have pledged to decolonize education, based upon one of ninety-four calls to action of the Truth and Reconciliation Commission.[9] Dean

Dori believes OCADU is serious about answering the call. We've met her boss, President and Vice-Chancellor Sara Diamond, in Chapter 3. So we know OCADU is serious about removing the barriers that keep the four groups designated by Canada's employment equity legislation—Indigenous peoples, persons of colour, creators with disabilities, and women—from being involved in art and design.

Not that it will be easy. At the time of my conversation with Dori, OCADU had no tenure track or tenured black faculty member in the Faculty of Design. Nor did it have an Indigenous one. This cannot continue, as Dori knows from her Australian experience. Thus, she has pledged herself to a ten-year stint at OCADU, two five-year terms. She is not moving for a substantial amount of time. Dori looks sad when she talks about the number of former deans of the Faculty of Design in the past ten years, almost a revolving door.[10]

Dori comes from an advantaged background in the United States. Her slave ancestry family, her great-grandmother Woods, had a homestead; actually the town where they lived was a black town in Indiana. When Dori's grandparents were still alive, they had regular family reunions of about eighty people. She says she can be in downtown Indianapolis today, and people will recognize her as belonging to the Woods family.

This substantial pedigree led Dori to a substantial education: Bryn Mawr College, then master's and doctorate degrees from Stanford University (1994–99) in anthropology. Her Ivy League education led to work experience at leading IT-design firms, E-Lab and then Cambridge-based Sapient Corporation. After stints at those dynamic firms, the academic and civic bug bit Dori, and in 2005 she was associate director, City Design Center, University of Illinois at Chicago, and associate professor of design anthropology. Perhaps her transition is understandable in view of the economics-only measurement of success of the leading IT-design firms. As Dori explained in a 2006 journal article,

> The economic downturn in the high-tech sector in the early 2000s ushered in a focus, by business decision-makers, nearly solely on economic performance. At places like Sapient, ethnographers were forced to adapt to the new business environment or were laid off. And adapting to the new business environment required not just learning the modalities of business, but co-participation in productive force through the packaging of ethnographically-informed service offerings. It is not an accident that my position at Arc Worldwide was one of experience planner not experience modeler or researcher. Some ethnographers were resistant to these processes for moral or economic reasons and opted out.[11]

By 2009, Dori wanted to work in senior academic administration and realized she had hit the race-tinted glass ceiling. Her family said, "Go wherever you need to go

to do whatever you need to do." The place with the opportunity turned out to be Australia, where she became associate dean of learning and teaching, Faculty of Design, and
associate professor of design anthropology at Swinburne
University of Technology in Melbourne.

In many ways, Australia was great preparation for
Canada. To cite the obvious, what stands out about
Australia is the large number of Indigenous people who are
increasingly decolonizing themselves in a Commonwealth
country that had both residential schools and reserves.
Dean Dori observes, as others have, that Australia learned
how to run residential schools from Canada. Australia's
bigger cities are increasingly home to immigrants from all
over the world. In Toronto, this all sounds familiar.

What does the process of decolonization mean for
design education? It means rejecting all objects, spaces,
and interactions created from the "modernist" project,
which erases cultural difference and believes in progress
through technology.

After seven years in Melbourne, Dori was ready to be
a dean of design on her home territory, the United States.
However, it wasn't ready for her. At least it wasn't ready
for her to be a dean of design at one of the top postsecondary schools. The job at OCADU was the eleventh one
for which she applied, and the yes came at a fortunate
moment as Dori saw it. She had been supporting Hillary
Clinton in her run for Democratic candidate and then
hopefully president of the United States. It had become

clear to Dori while working on the California campaign
that Hillary would not win, could not win. It was also clear
to her that she herself would not win, could not win, dean
of design in the United States.[12]

I've speculated for many years about why it is harder
for the four designated groups to get to the top in the representational professions, specifically the arts and cultural
industries. Put differently, why is it harder for individuals
in the four groups to be the artistic director of a major
theatre than the president of a bank? I believe that when
the artist (broadly defined) appears to say "I understand
all of you people who are not like me, and I can repre-
sent you," as opposed to just making money for you, it is
really threatening. Perhaps dean of design in a major art
and design institution is high up on the representational
scale. Design involves every object and reality we touch
and encounter, our whole world.

Neither Dori nor Secretary Clinton was able to make
it to the top of their symbolic professions in 2016 in the
United States. It was not ready for them. But Canada was
ready for a black female dean of design. OCADU, with Sara
Diamond as its president, was ready.

What does "decolonizing design" mean? A basic definition, says Dean Dori, is that in an educational setting
a student does not have to choose between her identity
and learning about/doing design. As long as students are
taught in the European mode, she asserts, they do have
to decide on one or the other. If the European identity

is the only one on offer and is necessary to work in the field, then students have to shed their actual identities. They have to shed black, Indigenous, Asian, Mexican, and other identities. Those identities don't count in a European-focused education.

What is striking about her many media appearances, scholarly and informal writing, and presentations at academic and industry conferences is how Dori talks to people about their complete world, all of which is touched by design. There is nothing airy-fairy or hopelessly theoretical about her personal or professional style. The dean is a down-to-earth black woman with an awareness of many cultures. "This isn't Europe," she states in the rap music and spoken word poetry that are parts of her communications portfolio.[13]

When asked about design anthropology, Dori responds passionately about "how participation in the design process empowers marginalized communities." Her plan is to prove that just as marginalized communities can lead in Australia so too can they lead in Canada at OCAD University. "Respectful design" is what she says is being defined, taught, and experienced at OCADU. When considering design curriculum, Dori asks, "Whose values are we actually prioritizing?" As long as Indigenous, black, and other non-settler students feel left out, they are being taught to give up their identities to be designers.

At OCADU, the faculty and new dean have been going through a process of defining and developing respectful design. It means more than one thing, says Dean Dori. The following statements arose out of a faculty workshop and now form the basis for what Dori says is the Faculty of Design's "ethos of Respectful Design":

> Respectful design means valuing inclusivity, people's cultures, and ways of knowing through empathic and responsible creative methodologies.
>
> It means deepening our relationships to the lives of the materials that connect us to the craft of making.
>
> It means designing ourselves back into the environment. For example, adding Indigenous concepts of Seven Generations to inform sustainable design.
>
> It means celebrating need over want.
>
> Respectful design means acknowledging different values, different manners of production, and different ways of knowing.[14]

Dori framed and described Design for Democracy, a graphic arts think tank in the US, where she had been Managing Director. She picked a provocative example from their work, the Internal Revenue Service (IRS). Dori consulted with the IRS on how it could communicate more productively. She asserted that the IRS could be described as the one place where the society had agreed on what it would provide for everyone. The IRS would collect the resources in order to provide for the common good of all. Those are the values in Design for

Democracy. Dori was deeply disturbed to have lived and worked in Australia for seven years and then to have gone back to the United States and found it the same, in fact worse. It was worse in its exclusionary thinking. She sees Design for Democracy as a substantial part of the cure for economic and democratic woes in the country: "In the United States, actions speak louder than words as robust design strategies are implemented independently by a spectrum of agencies, associations, and schools."[15] In these Trump years, something exciting is going on, very revolutionary, proclaimed Dori. What is energizing for her is the sheer level of resistance in the United States, at all levels up to the Trump administration.

Dean Dori is committed to OCADU until 2026, so the institution and the dean will have plenty of opportunities to transform each other. She is positive that design can be decolonized. Canada is giving her an opportunity to do so, one that she wouldn't have in any other country. And by 2026 perhaps the major postsecondary institutions of art and design in the United States will be ready for a black female dean. A ten-year commitment to Canada is significant.

"Why bother going back?" I asked Dori. She responded that what happens in the United States is important. It matters. Being part of the movement to transform the United States is in her civil rights DNA. Her ancestors expected her to play a significant role in the struggle. And if the country can be transformed, says

Dori, instead of being lethal to the rest of the world, it will be greatly beneficial.

Dori is confident. She is determined. I can only hope along with her that another ten years will make a huge dent in the colonizing stance of the United States.

EPILOGUE

BUILD ON IT

The "American refugees" profiled in this book all crossed the world's longest undefended border into Canada. They feared for their lives, or their political freedom, or the brutal destruction of their most cherished values and work, at times when that border was definitely being defended by the United States and sometimes by Canada. Canada made promises to them of a better present and a better future, and in many cases these promises were kept, at least some of the time. We can conclude that the promises were kept to individuals depending on larger Canadian and American policies and realities of the particular era, depending on the race and ethnicity of the individuals, and depending on the considerable discretion of border guards on both sides.

During the Revolutionary War and the War of 1812, Canada, for the most part, welcomed those loyal to the British crown. We might hear snickers now that some Loyalists arrived several years after the wars just to obtain land, but that was not the case with the Loyalists in this book. The United States was certainly fighting the British crown, so those were defended border times. The welcome was uneven for people of colour, and loyalty to Indigenous peoples—whose land it was anyway—was on and off again, mainly off. But still, Indigenous peoples and those of colour were loyal to the British crown.

There are significant ways in which all of the immigration/refugee stories told here are counter to the bigger narrative that we Canadians like to tell. First, our preferred story is that Canada always welcomes, and gives shelter to, those fleeing from some form of oppression in the United States: Canada is a sanctuary. Second, we like to think that the Canadian values of peacekeeping, fairness, and non-discrimination have been constant and unchanging throughout our history: Canada is peaceful and tolerant. Third, we picture that, in crossing the border into Canada, the refugee is protected by different laws in a sovereign country: Canadians are masters in their own house.

MY STORY CONTINUES: AMERICAN NO LONGER

My own deep personal and professional concerns focus on the Canadian values of diversity, equity, pluralism, and

Canadian content/sovereignty in arts and culture. I spoke on this topic in 2009 in the third annual Dr. Gail Guthrie Valaskakis Lecture on Diversity in Canadian Media for the Centre for Research-Action on Race Relations:

Who Will Inherit the Airwaves?

Build On It.

My father's family was from Jacksboro, Texas, a very small town 60 miles north of Fort Worth. There was a one-room Black school, where my Aunt Linnie Shelton was the teacher and principal. And there were two Black churches, Baptist and Methodist, both without regular preachers, visited by circuit riders, and where my Aunt Linnie was the superintendent of the Sunday School and ran everything.

Twenty-one years ago we had the last of the Shelton family reunions in Jacksboro. Months before the event I wrote from Regina, where we lived then, to my cousin, a medical doctor in Dallas who was the organizer of the reunion, and asked if there was anything we could help with. No, he said. Yet the night before the family reunion church service, it was clear that Aunt Linnie had failed to arrange for a preacher. She looked heavenward and said, "The Lord will provide, the preacher from furtherist away will preach." This was a veiled but obvious reference to my husband, Rex, a graduate of McMaster Divinity College, Union Theological Seminary in New York, and a full-time playwright.

When the family from Houston, Dallas, Los Angeles, et cetera—and Saskatchewan—packed into the tiny church, it was quite full. And there was an amazing gospel quartet from Mineral Wells, Texas. Strangely, as the service went on, other preachers appeared, sat on the platform, and then gave long resonant prayers.

Finally, the time for Rex's short-notice sermon arrived. He was very good, garnering many Amens, shouts, preach it brothers, and so forth. Then he delivered what I knew to be his final dazzling point, and one of the God's Trombone's basso profundo voices at the back, on the platform, encouraged him by intoning: "Amen! Now Build on it, Brother!!!"

Needless to say, this has been our family's key story for the twenty years since....We tell each other to "Build on It!"

Let us spend our few moments together on the concept of "Build on It" when it comes to ethnic and cultural diversity in Canadian media, Canadian television in particular in which I've spent 35 working years. We're talking about television as it is practised and experienced by the four designated groups...: women, Aboriginal peoples, persons with disabilities, and visible minority workers.[1]

In arts and cultural industries, we have achieved neither equity nor sovereignty. In 2018, one might even be considered naive to desire an equitable and sovereign outcome in Canadian media.

We immigrants and refugees from the United States are always trying to "build on it." For some, the legendary welcome to Canada, or inherent equality, has seldom been realized. For others, it has eventually worn off, usually because of changed policy circumstances with the United States. For yet others, seriously changed policy circumstances in Canada have made relative newcomers feel as though they are living with double standards. The freedoms and distinct Canadian virtues that American expats have cherished are in the process of changing. Yet, for all, many things are better.

The most recent wrinkle, discovering you are considered an Accidental American for US tax purposes, means either an expensive "renunciation" or a dual citizenship that might give duals the benefits of neither country. In August 2016, I received my Certificate of Loss of Nationality from the US Consulate nine months after applying for it and a year and a half after that US border guard surprised me in Miami with the news that I was "still an American." Washington, DC, agreed with me that I had in fact willingly relinquished American citizenship in 1975. This means that I am now officially not an American; I am a uni-citizen of Canada; I can travel to the United States on a Canadian passport like other Canadians (I think) and won't have my financial information transferred to the United States (I think). It's likely, however, that the post-Trump security concerns will continue to make travel from Canada to the United States less seamless.

The 2016 presidential election in the United States spawned many satirical comments about immigration to Canada or marriage to Canadians in the case (then thought unlikely) that the United States swung to the far isolationist and racist right. Commentators said that they had it wrong from the primaries through the election. It *was* possible, in fact, for the country to go completely to the anti-progressive right, to seek to build a nation without people of colour and immigrants, to build walls at its borders. Lady Liberty would no longer say,

> Give me your tired, your poor,
> Your huddled masses yearning to breathe free,
> The wretched refuse of your teeming shore.
> Send these, the homeless, tempest-tossed to me,
> I lift my lamp beside the golden door!

Many think that Canada, too, is not as welcoming today as it has been in the past, particularly in regards to Iraq War resisters. In an opinion piece for *NOW* magazine on Remembrance Day in 2015, John Hagan, co-director of the Center on Law and Globalization at the American Bar Foundation, recalled the famous words of Pierre Trudeau in opening the door to US Vietnam War resisters in 1969: "those who make the conscientious judgment that they must not participate in this war…have my complete sympathy, and indeed our political approach has been to give them access to Canada." Hagan went on to challenge

Prime Minister Justin Trudeau to "act now to reverse the harmful effects of a lost decade under Stephen Harper."[2]

In 2016, a number of groups—including Amnesty International Canada, the Canadian Council of Churches, and the Canadian Labour Congress—wrote to the Liberal government "in support of the Iraq War resisters' struggle to get permanent resident status."[3] These were joined by Vietnam War resisters, like those we met in Chapter 4, in calling for "Justin Trudeau to end the former Conservative government's efforts to deport American Iraq War resisters."[4] In essence, this coalition is asking for Canada to assert its sovereignty for this era's Iraq War resisters as it did for the 1960s Vietnam War resisters.

Indeed, Iraq War resisters have been deported from Canada to the United States. Some have served jail time. Many are remaining anonymous at this time because of the uncertainty of their status. And some have left underground Canada to become global underground nomads, as Iraq War resister Corey Glass wrote in *NOW* magazine in 2014:

> I will talk about what has happened to me since I quit the U.S. Army, went to Canada to escape the war and, after eight years trying to build a life there, was told I had to leave.
>
> After a very nice going-away/birthday party with friends…I packed for my indefinite vacation. (In eight years it's surprising how much stuff one person can

accumulate.) I decided to work my way east. After some heartfelt goodbyes, I boarded a plane to Ireland, where there's a sizable anti-war movement. Guess what other nation didn't send soldiers to Iraq?

I lived in dive bars covered with graffiti and was taken under the wing of a local activist who was frequently arrested trying to shut down Shannon Airport for flying American troops to Iraq…

Eventually, I would run out of savings and favours. I started to understand how easy it is for war vets to become homeless. Would this be me?…

I remembered losing friends back in the U.S. because of my choice to resist going back to war in Iraq.[5]

At this point in our alternative Canadian narrative, a small voice always asks, "But isn't Canada really a better society?" The answer is a strong "Yes—but with caveats."

Immigrants and refugees from the United States to Canada do not buy in to either/or thinking: either Canada is the best country in the world (that is, it has never done anything wrong), or Canada has made so many racist, sexist, classist, colonial mistakes that we might as well give up (that is, Canada is just as bad as the United States).

As of this writing, I have presided at seven citizenship ceremonies in the Greater Toronto Area. At those ceremonies, the majority of new citizens are brown, black, Asian, with a small number of white people who seem to be primarily Slavs/Ukrainians/Russians. Although the 25,000

Syrian refugees have not made it to citizenship court yet, Canada has admitted at least that many asylum seekers from a country banned by the United States.

New citizens are learning about a different Canadian reality. Near the beginning of the ceremony, we offer a treaty acknowledgement. And the Truth and Reconciliation Commission has called for an additional clause in the Oath of Citizenship:

> We call upon the Government of Canada to replace the Oath of Citizenship with the following: I swear (or affirm) that I will be faithful and bear true allegiance to Her Majesty Queen Elizabeth II, Queen of Canada, Her Heirs and Successors, and that I will faithfully observe the laws of Canada including Treaties with Indigenous Peoples, and fulfill my duties as a Canadian citizen.[6]

The fears of those early immigration officials are coming true, it appears. The white Protestant Canada is definitely disappearing. An evolved Canada is emerging. At a recent ceremony, where I was an observer, an Indigenous Elder said, "Paddle alongside me in your canoe. Find out about us. We have always welcomed you. And we still do."

For the American refugees and immigrants in this book, there are serious concerns about Canada *right now* that must be addressed. Their complex vision of Canada includes maintaining a vibrant universal health-care system; ensuring taxpayer support for the arts and cultural industries that foster Canadian content; seeking to be peacemakers, not warmongers, in the world, including welcoming resisters of the Iraq War and 25,000 Syrian refugees; and undertaking acknowledgement of, and restitution for, Canada's racist and colonial past and present (which apply most strongly to Indigenous peoples but also to persons of colour). That Canada is "better" on all these issues than the United States is why American expats have come here and stayed here. But better is not good enough. They are also activists who consider it their responsibility to help create improvements in Canadian society.

In spite of these difficulties, we born-again Canadians view Canada as the best country in the world. Mistakes have been made, and are being made now, that must be acknowledged. With full acknowledgement of them, Canada will keep moving toward that best-country label—and will even achieve it from time to time.

Without a doubt, the conservative rhetoric in the 2016 presidential election was about race, women, building walls at the borders, limiting or stopping the immigration of people of colour, banning Muslim immigration, waging war, and cancelling the modest Obamacare universal health plan. Race and war have been central factors in why American refugees have fled to Canada for more than 250 years, and once again race and war are behind the latest waves of American political refugees in Canada. This influx includes Iraq War resisters; those fleeing from Haiti, Somalia, and Ghana to avoid deportation; and dual

Canadian-American citizens who have decided to become un-American.

It is difficult to predict how many former residents of the United States will be standing in citizenship court as soon as they become eligible. Many, of course, are already Canadians and many are now applying for the Certificate of Loss of Nationality (like me). The number estimated to have renounced US citizenship in 2015 was up 43 percent over the number in 2014, and apparently the trend is continuing.[7] They are closing a door by choice.

Ten citizenship judges were appointed in spring 2018, in part because of a pressing need to deal with the backlog of new immigrants and refugees waiting to be sworn in.[8] People are lined up to swear allegiance to Queen Elizabeth II and all her heirs and successors. These judge positions had not been considered urgent vacancies for our federal government to fill. That changed. The need for wise citizenship judges has become glaringly urgent—again.

NOTES

INTRODUCTION

1 Justin Trudeau, "Statement by the Prime Minister of Canada on the Result of the US Presidential Election," Government of Canada website, November 9, 2016, https://pm.gc.ca/eng/news/2016/11/09/statement-prime-minister-canada-result-us-presidential-election.

2 USA for UNHCR, The UN Refugee Agency, "What is a Refugee?" Refugee Facts web page, https://www.unrefugees.org/refugee-facts/what-is-a-refugee/.

3 Elizabeth Thompson, "Revenue Canada Quietly Handed 155,000 Canadian Banking Records to IRS," *iPolitics*, March 16, 2016, https://ipolitics.ca/2016/03/16/revenue-canada-quietly-handed-155000-canadian-banking-records-to-irs/.

4 Rita Shelton Deverell, *Smoked Glass Ceiling*, copy script (Toronto: Playwrights Guild of Canada, 2006), 1.

1. OPENING SNAPSHOTS

1 Norman Knowles, *Inventing the Loyalists: The Ontario Loyalist Tradition and the Creation of Usable Pasts* (Toronto: University of Toronto Press, 1997), 161, 166.

2   Pat Kennedy, personal communication, May 2016, referring
    to Phillip W. Hoffman, *Simon Girty, Turncoat Hero: The Most
    Hated Man on the Early American Frontier* (Staunton, VA:
    American History Press, 2009), https://www.amazon.ca/
    Simon-Girty-Turncoat-Phillip-Hoffman/dp/0984225633. From
    publicity for the book: "After defecting from the Patriot cause
    to serve the British in March 1778, Girty achieved instant
    infamy. To understand his motivation one must discover, as he
    did, that the real, underlying cause of the American Revolution
    was the unquenchable thirst for Indian land of many of our
    so-called founding fathers—including George Washington—
    and their unrelenting dissatisfaction with the restrictions
    imposed upon their land speculation ambitions by the King's
    Proclamation of 1763."

3   Stephen Vincent Benét, "The Devil and Daniel Webster," http://
    fullreads.com/literature/the-devil-and-daniel-webster/5/, 5.

4   https://www.amazon.ca/Simon-Girty-Turncoat-Phillip-Hoffman/
    dp/0984225633.

5   William R. Wilson, "Simon Girty: History's Realities Are
    Seldom Dull," *Historical Narratives of Early Canada*, http://www.
    uppercanadahistory.ca/ttuc/ttuc7.html.

6   "Syncrude Award for Excellence in Sustainable Development—
    Description," *The Canadian Institute of Mining, Metallurgy, and
    Petroleum*, http://web.cim.org/awards/syncrude.cfm.

7   Pat Kennedy, personal communication, May 2016.

2. CANADIAN LOYALTY TESTED

1   "Keenagers Year-End Event," *Emmanuel News and Notes*,
    June 2013, http://emmanuelpresbyterian.ca/files/2011/09/
    Newsletter-2013-06.pdf.

2   Judy Plaxton, "Lives Lived," *Globe and Mail*, May 15, 2015,
    https://www.theglobeandmail.com/life/facts-and-arguments/
    lives-lived-wilfred-joseph-theodore-sheffield-96/article24436004/.

3   Naomi Norquay, interview with Carolynn Wilson, *Northern Terminus: The African Canadian History Journal*, Vol. 8, 2011, 4–12, https://greyroots.com/sites/default/files/naomi_norquay_interview_with_carolynn_wilson_2011.pdf.

4   Oro African Methodist Episcopal Church facebook post, August 10, 2016.

5   Dana Flavelle Economy, "Fundraiser for Black Church Unites Community," *Toronto Star*, May 3, 2015, https://www.thestar.com/news/gta/2015/05/03/fundraiser-for-black-church-unites-community.html.

6   John Merritt, "Remembering the Past, Legitimizing the Present: The Campaigns to Preserve the African Methodist Episcopal Church in Oro Township and Canadian Social Memory in the 1940s and the Present Day" (MA thesis, School of Graduate Studies, Laurentian University, 2015), 3. Reprinted with permission of the author.

7   Ibid., 3–4.

8   Ibid., 6.

9   Ibid., 7.

10   Ibid.

11   "The Wilson Incident," *In Focus* (Rogers Television series), 2017, https://www.youtube.com/watch?v=m6GrxGeFkFY.

12   Sylvia and Carolynn Wilson, conversation with the author, 2016.

13   Sylvia D. Hamilton's awards include a Gemini, the Portia White Prize, the CBC Television Pioneer Award, and the Queen's Diamond Jubilee Medal. She worked with the National Film Board's Studio D (The Women's Studio), where she co-created New Initiatives in Film, a program for women of colour and First Nations women. For a more complete summary of Sylvia's contributions and accolades, see "Sylvia D. Hamilton: Assistant Professor, Rogers Chair in Communications," *University of King's College*, https://ukings.ca/people/sylvia-d-hamilton/.

14   "Sylvia Hamilton Traces Her Roots in New Poetry Collection," January 12, 2016, *The Next Chapter*, with Shelagh Rogers, CBC

Radio, http://www.cbc.ca/radio/thenextchapter/brian-francis-tests-3-diet-books-and-sylvia-hamilton-explores-her-african-canadian-roots-1.3392199/sylvia-hamilton-traces-her-roots-in-new-poetry-collection-1.3392556.

15 Sylvia D. Hamilton, "Stories from *The Little Black School House*," in *Cultivating Canada: Reconciliation through the Lens of Cultural Diversity*, Aboriginal Healing Foundation Research Series 3, ed. Ashok Mathur, Jonathan Dewar, and Mike DeGagne (Ottawa: Aboriginal Healing Foundation, 2011), 91–112. Excerpt reprinted with permission of the author.

16 Ibid., 99.

17 Pamela Edmonds, "Mining Memory: Sylvia D. Hamilton's Art of Telling History," *Excavation: A Site of Memory*, exhibition catalogue (Halifax: Dalhousie University Art Gallery, October 18–December 1, 2013), 7.

18 Maritime Museum of the Atlantic, "Excavation: A Site of Memory," What to See & Do, October 30 to November 30, 2014, https://maritimemuseum.novascotia.ca/what-see-do/excavation-site-memory.

19 Sylvia D. Hamilton, "Notes for a Talk: *Excavation: A Site of Memory*, Maritime Museum of the Atlantic," November 6, 2014, https://maroonfilmsinc.wordpress.com/2014/11/17/notes-for-a-talk-excavation-a-site-of-memory-maritime-museum-of-the-atlantic/.

20 Chris Cornish, "Sylvia Hamilton Talks about Writing *And I Alone Escaped to Tell You*," *yFile: York University's News*, December 15, 2014, http://yfile.news.yorku.ca/2014/12/15/sylvia-hamilton-talks-about-writing-and-i-alone-escaped-to-tell-you.

21 Michael Dennis, review of *And I Alone Escaped to Tell You*, by Sylvia D. Hamilton, *Today's Book of Poetry*, October 27, 2014, http://michaeldennispoet.blogspot.ca/2014/10/and-i-alone-escaped-to-tell-you-sylvia.html.

22 Sylvia D. Hamilton, *And I Alone Escaped to Tell You* (Kentville, NS: Gaspereau Press, 2014), 22. Reprinted with permission of the author and the publisher.

23 Ibid., 94.

24 Hilary Beaumont, "Black Nova Scotians Might Finally Own the Land They've Lived On for Generations," *Vice News*, September 28, 2017, https://news.vice.com/en_ca/article/a3j4vb/black-nova-scotians-might-finally-own-the-land-t-lived-on-for-generations.

25 Robin Winks, *The Blacks in Canada* (Montreal: McGill-Queen's University Press, 1997), 288–336.

26 Eli Yarhi, "Order-in-Council P.C. 1911-1324—The Proposed Ban on Black Immigration to Canada," *The Canadian Encyclopedia*, https://thecanadianencyclopedia.ca/en/article/order-in-council-pc-1911-1324-the-proposed-ban-on-black-immigration-to-canada/.

27 "Descendants of Saskatchewan's Original Black Settlers," *Oral History Centre*, http://oralhistorycentre.ca/fonds/descendants-saskatchewans-original-black-settlers.

28 Charlotte Mayes Williams, conversation with the author, December 2017.

29 See "Klan Plans Fall Rally in Sask., Says Leader," *CBC News*, August 27, 2007, http://www.cbc.ca/news/canada/saskatchewan/klan-plans-fall-rally-in-sask-says-leader-1.690030; and Kendall Latimer, "KKK History Challenges Idea Sask. Always Welcomed Newcomers: Expert," *CBC News*, August 18, 2017, http://www.cbc.ca/news/canada/saskatchewan/ku-klux-klan-saskatchewan-history-1.4251309.

30 Charlotte Mayes Williams, conversation with the author, December 2017.

31 https://admissions.usask.ca/documents/brochures/vetmed.pdf, 10.

32 Charlotte Mayes Williams, conversation with the author, December 2017.

33 https://admissions.usask.ca/documents/brochures/vetmed.pdf, 10.

34 Sophie McCall, "Grey Owl's Wife: A New Biography Brings This Fiercely Free Spirit to the Fore," review of *Anahareo: A Wilderness Spirit*, by Kristin Gleeson, *Literary Review of Canada*, reviewcanada.ca/magazine/2013/07/grey-owls-wife/.

35 Grant MacEwan, "Sitting Bull," *The Canadian Encyclopedia*, http://thecanadianencyclopedia.ca/en/article/sitting-bull/.

36 Stuart R. J. Sutherland, "Jay's Treaty," *The Canadian Encyclopedia*,
    http://thecanadianencyclopedia.ca/en/article/jays-treaty/.

37 Rita Shelton Deverell, "Slavery Endangers the Masters' Health,
    but Please Don't Shoot the Messenger," in *Cultivating Canada:
    Reconciliation through the Lens of Cultural Diversity*, Aboriginal
    Healing Foundation Research Series 3, ed. Ashok Mathur,
    Jonathan Dewar, and Mike DeGagne (Ottawa: Aboriginal Healing
    Foundation, 2011), 385–86.

38 Dan David, conversation with and email to the author, 2017.

39 Dan David, "Behind the Lines: Invisible Scars Left by Oka Crisis
    25 Years Later: Mohawk Journalist Dan David Reflects on His
    Time during Oka Summer." *CBC News*, updated July 17, 2015,
    http://www.cbc.ca/news/indigenous/behind-the-lines-invisible-
    scars-left-by-oka-crisis-25-years-later-1.3145297. Used with
    permission.

40 Dan David, email to the author, 2016.

41 Dan David, "All My Relations," *Taking Risks: Literary Journalism
    from the Edge,* ed. Barbara Moon and Don Obe (Banff: Banff
    Centre Press, 1998), 52.

42 Ibid., 57.

43 Ibid., 58–59.

44 Negotiating the Canada-US border, for Indigenous people and
    for others of colour, is never straightforward, and has become
    even more difficult since 9/11. See, for example, Renée K. Gadoua,
    "Passport Impasse Blocks Haudenosaunee Lacrosse Team,"
    Syracuse New Times, July 29, 2015, https://www.syracusenewtimes.
    com/passport-impasse-blocks-haudenosaunee-lacrosse-team/.
    The Haudenosaunee Nation Women's Lacrosse under-19 team was
    refused entry to the United Kingdom under their Haudenosaunee
    passports.

45 Dan David, email to the author, 2015.

46 Dan David, conversation with and email to the author, 2016.

3. AMERICAN LOYALTY TESTED

1   Deverell, *Smoked Glass Ceiling*, 2.

2   Ibid., 4.

3   Ibid., 11.

4   As quoted in Daisy Bates, *Daisy Bates, a Memoir: The Long Shadow of Little Rock* (New York: David McKay, 1962), 70–71; for other accounts of events that day, see "One of the 'Little Rock' Nine Looks Back," *National Public Radio*, September 4, 2007, https://www.npr.org/templates/transcript/transcript. php?storyId=14091050; and Monica Haberny, "Women of the Past and Present Shaping the Future," *Archives and Public History at UMass Boston*, March 27, 2017, http://www.archivespublichistory. org/?tag=grace-lorch.

5   Anna St. Onge, "Black History Month Featured Fonds: Lee and Grace Lorch," *News from the Clara Thomas Archives and Special Collections*, February 24, 2012, http://deantiquate.blog.yorku. ca/2012/02/24/bhm2012_leeandgracelorch/.

6   Anthony B. Newkirk, "Grace Lonergan Lorch (1903–1974)," *The Encyclopedia of Arkansas History and Culture*, http:// www.encyclopediaofarkansas.net/encyclopedia/entry-detail. aspx?entryID=8397.

7   Matthew Behrens, "Daughters of the Blacklist: Why *Trumbo* Hits Home," *NOW*, December 16, 2015, https://nowtoronto.com/news/ daughters-of-the-blacklist-trumbo-hits-home/.

8   Amy Cohen-Corwin, "Yueh-Gin Gung and Dr. Charles Y. Hu Award to Lee Lorch for Distinguished Service to Mathematics," March 2007, https://www.maa.org/sites/default/files/pdf/pubs/ Lorch_Monthly.pdf; see also John Dupuis, "Mathematician and Activist Lee Lorch, 1915–2014," March 17, 2014, http://scienceblogs. com/confessions/2014/03/17/mathematician-and-activist-lee- lorch-1915-2014/.

9   Rachel Deutsch, "Conversations with Lee Lorch," *Science for Peace*, June 5, 2013, https://www.youtube.com/watch?v=x3MKhuuMhE0.

10   "Majority of Canadians Want Iraq War Resisters to Stay as
     Permanent Residents," *War Resisters Support Campaign*, June 13,
     2016, http://resisters.ca/.

11   Florence Bean James (with Jean Freeman), *Fists Upon A Star: A
     Memoir of Love, Theatre, and Escape from McCarthyism* (Regina:
     University of Regina Press, 2013), 5.

12   "Rita Deverell Fought Her Way on Stage—and 50 Years Later,
     She's Still Fighting," *Up Close: A Special Series*, with Lyndie
     Greenwood, CBC Radio, July 16, 2017, http://www.cbc.ca/radio/
     docproject/upclose/rita-deverell-fought-her-way-on-stage-and-
     50-years-later-she-s-still-fighting-1.4207626.

13   Mavor Moore, "Theatre Pioneer Was a Welcome U.S. Invader,"
     Obituary of Florence Bean James, *Globe and Mail*, February 13,
     1988, E1. Used with permission.

14   Rita Shelton Deverell, *McCarthy and the Old Woman*, full-length
     copy script (Toronto: Playwrights Guild of Canada, 2008), 2–3.

15   Ibid., 15–16.

16   Rita Shelton Deverell, "Epilogue," in *Fists Upon a Star: A Memoir of
     Love, Theatre, and Escape from McCarthyism*, by Florence Bean James
     with Jean Freeman (Regina: University of Regina Press, 2013), 249–51,
     255, 259. Italicized text is from Florence Bean James, audio-taped
     conversations with the author, Regina, 1976–77, https://www.uregina.
     ca/library/services/archives/collections/writing-theatre/deverell-
     rita.html. The report of Burton James's death is from Saskatchewan
     Arts Board, *Annual Report of the Saskatchewan Arts Board to the
     Legislature*, 1952, 12, Provincial Archives of Saskatchewan.

17   Ibid., 260.

18   Mavor Moore, "Theatre Pioneer."

19   Rita Shelton Deverell, "Speak UP: The Story of Florence James and
     Her Fight against McCarthyism," unpublished screenplay, 2016.

20   "About Dr. Sara Diamond: A Brief Biographical Note: Dr. Sara
     Diamond, OCAD University President," *OCAD University*, http://
     www.ocadu.ca/about/president/about.htm#sthash.5ltkAiac.dpuf.

21   Sara Diamond, email to the author, December 2017.

22 Sara Diamond, conversations with the author, 2015, 2016.

23 Sara Diamond, interview in Carol Whiteman, "Creating Space for Authentic Voice in Canada's Screen Industry" (EdD diss., Simon Fraser University, 2018).

24 http://www.widc.ca/.

25 "Toronto's Most Influential, the People Who Changed the City in 2014," *Toronto Life*, November 14, 2014, https://torontolife.com/city/toronto-most-influential-2014/

26 "Mrs. Mary Swit Diamond, Ex-Aide of Youth Board, 52," *New York Times*, March 30, 1964, http://www.nytimes.com/1964/03/30/mrs-mary-swit-diamond-exaide-of-youth-board-52.html.

27 Jean Gagnon, *Sara Diamond: mémoires ravivées, histoire narrée / Memories Revisited, History Retold* (Ottawa: Musée des beaux-arts du Canada / National Gallery of Canada, 1992), 47–51.

28 Truth and Reconciliation Commission, *Truth and Reconciliation Commission of Canada: Calls to Action* (Winnipeg: TRC, 2015), http://www.trc.ca/websites/trcinstitution/File/2015/Findings/Calls_to_Action_English2.pdf, 7 (Call 62).

29 Chris Rattan, "The Plan to Decolonize Design," *NOW*, August 30, 2017, https://nowtoronto.com/art-and-books/art/the-plan-to-decolonize-design/.

30 Ibid.

31 Rina Fraticelli, "Women in View," October 21, 2015, http://womeninview.ca/wp-content/uploads/2016/01/Women-In-View-On-Screen-2015.pdf; "Global Women's March Reignites on Trump Inauguration Anniversary to Protest against Policies and Support #MeToo," *Province*, January 20, 2018, http://theprovince.com/news/world/across-the-globe-rallies-against-trump-sexual-misconduct/wcm/a58477ae-81f6-4549-a730-2571970c615d.

4. FACES TURNED TOWARD CANADA

1   John Hagan, *Northern Passage: American Vietnam War Resisters in Canada* (Cambridge, MA: Harvard University Press, 2001), xi, xii.

2   Mary Jo Leddy, "Why Are We Here? A Meditation on Canada,"
    paper presented at the Catholic Health Alliance Conference,
    Charlottetown, May 10, 2017, 13, http://www.accs.ca/conference/
    pastconferences/2017/docs/Mary Jo Leddy Why Are We Here_A
    Meditation on Canada.pdf.

3   Jessica Squires, *Building Sanctuary: The Movement to Support
    Vietnam War Resisters in Canada, 1965–73* (Vancouver: UBC
    Press, 2013).

4   Deverell, *Smoked Glass Ceiling*, 6.

5   See Daniel Francis, "Stephen Leacock's Dark Side: The Famed
    Writer Sure Was a Funny Guy. And a Misogynist Racist,"
    review of *Stephen Leacock*, by Margaret MacMillan, *Geist
    Magazine*, August 23, 2010, https://thetyee.ca/Books/2010/08/23/
    StephenLeacock/.

6   Craig Dotson, "Family Matters," letter to his children, Christmas
    2006. The following quotations are also from this letter.

7   Craig Dotson, audiotaped conversation with the author, Regina,
    1980. The following quotations are also from this conversation.

8   Memory McLeod, "Dotson Was Dedicated to Learning, Public
    Life," *Leader-Post* (Regina), September 10, 2008, https://www.
    pressreader.com/canada/regina-leader-post/20080910/
    281590941366867.

9   Joanne Tompkins, conversation with the author, 2014.

10 "The LeBlanc and MacLean Families of Nova Scotia," obituary of
    Ed Miller, *rootsweb*, July 21, 2003, https://wc.rootsweb.ancestry.
    com/cgi-bin/igm.cgi?op=GET&db=tleblanc&id=I25389.

11 Joanne Tompkins, email to the author, August 2016. The following
    quotations are also from that email.

12 Roger Neville Williams, *The New Exiles: American War Resisters
    in Canada* (New York: Liveright Publishers, 1971), 58.

13 Hagan, *Northern Passage*, 126, 133–34.

14 Tompkins, email to the author, August 2016.

15 Tompkins, email to the author, August 2016. The following
    quotations are also from that email.

16   Joanne Tompkins, quoted in "StFX Education Students, High
     School Students Move towards Reconciliation, Use Art as
     a Vehicle for Social Change," *St. Francis Xavier University*,
     November 14, 2016, https://www.stfx.ca/about/news/students-
     learn-from-Aboriginal-leaders.

17   Conversations with Michael Klein and Bonnie Sherr Klein, 2016.

18   Tom Sito, "The Disney Strike of 1941: How It Changed
     Animation and Comics," Animation World Network (awn.
     com), July 19, 2005, https://www.awn.com/animationworld/
     disney-strike-1941-how-it-changed-animation-comics.

19   Bonnie Sherr Klein, "'Fierce Canadian' Fears for Her Country,"
     Tyee, May 27, 2013, https://thetyee.ca/Opinion/2013/05/27/
     Bonnie-Klein/.

20   Conversations with Michael Klein and Bonnie Sherr Klein, 2016.

21   Fifty years later, according to the PBS, the search for racial
     equality of opportunity is still evasive in Rochester. *Race Riots 50
     Years Later*, PBS, August 8, 2014.

22   Klein, "'Fierce Canadian.'"

23   Citation for investing Michael Klein as a Member of the Order
     of Canada, *The Governor General of Canada: His Excellency the
     Right Honourable David Johnston*, May 12, 2017, http://www.gg.ca/
     honour.aspx?id=4551&t=12&ln=Klein.

24   "The National Film Board of Canada Presents *Not a Love Story:
     A Film about Pornography*," http://www.onf-nfb.gc.ca/sg/100220.
     pdf.

25   Bonnie Sherr Klein, email to the author, 2016.

26   "Kickstart: Disability Arts and Culture," *International Centre
     of Art for Social Change*, https://www.icasc.ca/directory/
     kickstart-disability-arts-culture.

27   See Andy Barrie, "Trudeau Can Stop Harper's Vendetta Against
     Conscientious Objectors, *The Star* (Toronto), May 17, 2016, https://
     www.thestar.com/opinion/commentary/2016/05/17/trudeau-can-
     stop-harpers-vendetta-against-conscientious-objectors.html.

28   Klein, "'Fierce Canadian.'"

29 Steven Bush, conversations with the author, 2017.

30 Bush, conversation with the author, May 26, 2017.

31 "Parkdale Rent Strike Ends in Victory!," *Parkdale Organize*,
    August 3, 2017, http://parkdaleorganize.ca/2017/08/03/
    parkdale-rent-strike-ends-in-victory/.

32 Steven Bush, *Beating the Bushes* (Vancouver: Talonbooks, 2010),
    16–21.

33 Steven Bush, email to the author, June 20, 2017.

34 Frank Canino, "Two Holidays," unpublished play script, 2016, 3–4.

35 Frank Canino, conversation with the author, May 1, 2017.

36 Canino, "Two Holidays," 87–88.

37 Ibid.

5. CLOSING SNAPSHOTS

1   According to Wikipedia, same-gender marriage was legally
    recognized in the provinces and territories as of the following dates:

- June 10, 2003: Ontario
- July 8, 2003: British Columbia
- March 19, 2004: Quebec
- July 14, 2004: Yukon
- September 16, 2004: Manitoba
- September 24, 2004: Nova Scotia
- November 5, 2004: Saskatchewan
- December 21, 2004: Newfoundland and Labrador
- June 23, 2005: New Brunswick
- July 20, 2005 (Civil Marriage Act): Alberta, Prince
  Edward Island, Nunavut, and the Northwest
  Territories

Note that, in some of these cases, marriages were in fact legal
at earlier dates (e.g., the Ontario ruling held that marriages
performed in January 2001 were legal when performed), but the
legality was questioned. As of the given dates, the legality was
authoritatively established.

The decision by the Ontario government to recognize the marriage that took place in Toronto on January 14, 2001, retroactively made Canada the first country in the world to have a government-legitimized same-sex marriage (the Netherlands and Belgium, which legalized same-sex marriage before Canada did, had their first marriages in April 2001 and June 2003, respectively).

2   Deana Dudley, "Love Makes the World Go Round," sermon summary, Metropolitan Community Church, Toronto, July 6, 2015, http://www.mcctoronto.com/wp-content/uploads/images/AM-Sunday-news-07-12-15.pdf.

3   Ibid.

4   "Toronto Police Chief Mark Saunders Apologizes for 1981 Gay Bathhouse Raids," with files from CP, CBC News, June 22, 2016, http://www.cbc.ca/news/canada/toronto/police-apology-raids-1.3647668.

5   "Canada-U.S. Safe Third Country Agreement," Government of Canada, https://www.canada.ca/en/immigration-refugees-citizenship/corporate/mandate/policies-operational-instructions-agreements/agreements/safe-third-country-agreement.html#toc3.

6   Sunny Dhillon and Sean Fine, "Quebec and Manitoba See Influx of Asylum Seekers Crossing U.S. Border," Globe and Mail, February 12, 2017, https://www.theglobeandmail.com/news/national/quebec-and-manitoba-see-influx-of-asylum-seekers-crossing-us-border/article33995516/.

7   "HIRC Releases Report on Effect of Executive Orders on Refugees; Urges Canada to Reconsider Safe Third Country Agreement," Harvard Immigration and Refugee Clinical Program, https://harvardimmigrationclinic.wordpress.com/2017/02/08/hirc-releases-report-on-effect-of-executive-orders-on-refugees-urges-canada-to-reconsider-safe-third-country-agreement/.

8   "History," OCAD University, https://www.ocadu.ca/about/history.htm.

9   Truth and Reconciliation Commission, Truth and Reconciliation Commission of Canada: Calls to Action (Winnipeg: TRC, 2015),

        http://www.trc.ca/websites/trcinstitution/File/2015/Findings/
        Calls_to_Action_English2.pdf, 7 (Call 62).

10   Dori Tunstall, conversation with the author, December 2017.

11   Elizabeth (Dori) Tunstall, "The Yin and Yang of Seduction and
        Production: Social Transitions of Ethnography between Seductive
        Play and Productive Force in Industry," *Ethnographic Praxis in
        Industry Conference Proceedings* 1 (2006): 125–37, ISSN 1559-890X,
        http://openresearch.ocadu.ca/id/eprint/1264/1/Tunstall_Yin_
        2006.pdf.

12   Tunstall, conversation with the author, December 2017.

13   Elizabeth (Dori) Tunstall, "AIGA Respectful Design Video," *YouTube*,
        October 17, 2016, https://www.youtube.com/watch?v=sESVWI5aAHA;
        Dori Tunstall, "US Design Policy," *YouTube*, March 15, 2009,
        https://www.youtube.com/watch?v=aSczizV8Eqc&spfreload=10.

14   Dori Tunstall, "Dean Dori Tunstall on Respectful Design," *In
        Studio* (OCAD University), https://www2.ocadu.ca/feature/
        dean-dori-tunstall-on-respectful-design.

15   Elizabeth (Dori) Tunstall and Casey Jones, "Beyond the Document:
        Living Institutions of US National Design Policy," *Design
        Management Review* 21, 4 (2010): 16, ISSN 15570614, http://
        openresearch.ocadu.ca/id/eprint/1279/1/Tunstall_Beyond_2010.pdf.

EPILOGUE

1   Rita Shelton Deverell, "Who Will Inherit the Airwaves?,"
        Canadian Journal of Communication 34, 1 (2009): 143–44.

2   John Hagan, "For Iraq War Resisters, It's Vietnam All Over Again:
        Why Trudeau Must Act Now to Reverse Harper's Prosecution of
        U.S. Objectors in Canada," *NOW*, November 11, 2015, https://
        nowtoronto.com/news/for-iraq-war-resisters-it%E2%80%99s-
        vietnam-all-over-again/.

3   "Andy Barrie Asks Trudeau to Stop Harper's Vendetta Against
        Conscientious Objectors," *Market Wired*, May 17, 2016, http://

www.marketwired.com/press-release/andy-barrie-asks-trudeau-to-stop-harpers-vendetta-against-conscientious-objectors-2125795.htm.

4   Ibid.

5   Corey Glass, "Corey Glass: A War Resister's Story," *NOW*,
     December 17, 2014, https://nowtoronto.com/topics/corey-glass/.

6   Truth and Reconciliation Commission, *Truth and Reconciliation
     Commission of Canada: Calls to Action* (Winnipeg: TRC, 2015),
     http://www.trc.ca/websites/trcinstitution/File/2015/Findings/
     Calls_to_Action_English2.pdf, 11 (Call 94).

7   Barry McKenna, "Delays, Costs Mount for Canadians
     Renouncing U.S. Citizenship," *Globe and Mail*, updated March
     25, 2017, https://www.theglobeandmail.com/news/politics/
     delays-costs-mount-for-canadians-renouncing-us-citizenship/
     article28688026/.

8   Government of Canada. Immigration, Refugees, and Citizenship
     Canada. May 17, 2018, https://www.canada.ca/en/immigration-
     refugees-citizenship/news/2018/05/minister-hussen-announces-
     the-appointment-of-10-citizenship-judges.html.

SELECTED REFERENCES

"Andy Barrie Asks Trudeau to Stop Harper's Vendetta Against Conscientious Objectors." *Market Wired*. May 17, 2016. http://www.marketwired.com/press-release/andy-barrie-asks-trudeau-to-stop-harpers-vendetta-against-conscientious-objectors-2125795.htm.

Barrie, Andy. "Trudeau Can Stop Harper's Vendetta Against Conscientious Objectors." *The Star* (Toronto). May 17, 2016. https://www.thestar.com/opinion/commentary/2016/05/17/trudeau-can-stop-harpers-vendetta-against-conscientious-objectors.html.

Bates, Daisy. *Daisy Bates, a Memoir: The Long Shadow of Little Rock*. New York: David McKay, 1962.

Behrens, Matthew. "Daughters of the Blacklist: Why *Trumbo* Hits Home." *NOW*, December 16, 2015. https://nowtoronto.com/news/daughters-of-the-blacklist-trumbo-hits-home/.

Benét, Stephen Vincent. "The Devil and Daniel Webster." http://fullreads.com/literature/the-devil-and-daniel-webster/5/.

Bush, Steven. *Beating the Bushes*. Vancouver: Talonbooks, 2010.

Canino, Frank. "Two Holidays." Unpublished theatre script, 2016.

Cohen-Corwin, Amy. "Yueh-Gin Gung and Dr. Charles Y. Hu Award to Lee Lorch for Distinguished Service to Mathematics." March 2007. https://www.maa.org/sites/default/files/pdf/pubs/Lorch_Monthly.pdf.

Cornish, Chris. "Sylvia Hamilton Talks about Writing *And I Alone Escaped to Tell You. yFile: York University's News.* December 15, 2014. http://yfile.news.yorku.ca/2014/12/15/sylvia-hamilton-talks-about-writing-and-i-alone-escaped-to-tell-you.

David, Dan. "All My Relations." In *Taking Risks: Literary Journalism from the Edge*, edited by Barbara Moon and Don Oboe, 33–59. Banff: Banff Centre Press, 1998.

———. Blog. https://shmohawk.wordpress.com/.

Dennis, Michael. Review of *And I Alone Escaped to Tell You*, by Sylvia D. Hamilton. *Today's Book of Poetry*, October 27, 2014. http://michaeldennispoet.blogspot.ca/2014/10/and-i-alone-escaped-to-tell-you-sylvia.html.

Depuis, John. "Mathematician and Activist Lee Lorch, 1915–2014." March 17, 2014. http://scienceblogs.com/confessions/2014/03/17/mathematician-and-activist-lee-lorch-1915-2014.

Deutsch, Rachel. "Conversations with Lee Lorch." *Science for Peace*, June 5, 2013. https://www.youtube.com/watch?v=x3MKhuuMhEo.

Deverell, Rita Shelton. "Epilogue." In *Fists Upon a Star: Memoir of Love, Theatre, and Escape from McCarthyism*, by Florence Bean James and Jean Freeman, 237–58. Regina: University of Regina Press, 2013.

———. *McCarthy and the Old Woman*. Play for two actors. Toronto: Playwrights Guild of Canada, 2008.

———. "Slavery Endangers the Masters' Health, but Please Don't Shoot the Messenger." In *Cultivating Canada:*

Reconciliation through the Lens of Cultural Diversity, edited by Ashok Mathur, Jonathan Dewar, and Mike DeGagne, 383–95. Ottawa: Aboriginal Healing Foundation, 2011.

———. *Smoked Glass Ceiling*. One-woman show. Toronto: Playwrights Guild of Canada, 2006.

———. "Speak UP: The Story of Florence James and Her Fight against McCarthyism." Unpublished screenplay, 2016.

———. "Who Will Inherit the Airwaves?" Speech. *Canadian Journal of Communications* 34 (2009): 143–54.

Dudley, Deana. "Love Makes the World Go Round." Sermon, Metropolitan Community Church, Toronto, July 6, 2015. http://www.mcctoronto.com/wp-content/uploads/images/AM-SUNDAY-NEWS-07-12-15.pdf.

Economy, Dana Flavelle. "Fundraiser for Black Church Unites Community." *Toronto Star*, May 3, 2015. https://www.thestar.com/news/gta/2015/05/03/fundraiser-for-black-church-unites-community.html.

Edmonds, Pamela. "Mining Memory: Sylvia D. Hamilton's Art of Telling History."*Excavation: A Site of Memory*. Exhibition catalogue. Halifax: Dalhousie University Art Gallery, 2013.

Francis, Daniel. "Stephen Leacock's Dark Side: The Famed Writer Sure Was a Funny Guy. And a Misogynist Racist." Review of *Stephen Leacock*, by Margaret MacMillan. *Geist Magazine*, August 23, 2010. https://thetyee.ca/Books/2010/08/23/StephenLeacock/.

Fraticelli, Rina. "Women in View." October 21, 2015. http://womeninview.ca/wp-content/uploads/2016/01/Women-In-View-On-Screen-2015.pdf.

Gagnon, Jean. *Sara Diamond: mémoires ravivées, histoire narrée/Memories Revisited, History Retold*. Ottawa: Musée des beaux-arts du Canada/National Gallery of Canada, 1992: 47–51.

Glass, Corey. "Corey Glass: A War Resister's Story." *NOW*, December 17, 2014. https://nowtoronto.com/topics/corey-glass/.

Hagan, John. "For Iraq War Resisters, It's Vietnam All Over Again: Why Trudeau Must Act Now to Reverse Harper's Prosecution of U.S. Objectors in Canada." *NOW*, November 11, 2015. https://nowtoronto.com/news/for-iraq-war-resisters-it%E2%80%99s-vietnam-all-over-again.

———. *Northern Passage: American Vietnam War Resisters in Canada*. Cambridge, MA: Harvard University Press, 2001.

Hamilton, Sylvia D. *And I Alone Escaped to Tell You*. Kentville, NS: Gaspereau Press, 2014.

———. *Excavation: A Site of Memory*. Exhibition catalogue. Halifax: Maritime Museum of the Atlantic, 2015.

———. "Notes for a Talk: *Excavation: A Site of Memory*, Maritime Museum of the Atlantic." November 6, 2014. https://maroonfilmsinc.wordpress.com/2014/11/17/notes-for-a-talk-excavation-a-site-of-memory-maritime-museum-of-the-atlantic/.

———. *The Little Black School House*. Maroon Films, 2007.

———. "Stories from *The Little Black School House*." In *Cultivating Canada: Reconciliation through the Lens of Cultural Diversity*, edited by Ashok Mathur, Jonathan Dewar, and Mike DeGagne, 91–112. Ottawa: Aboriginal Healing Foundation, 2011.

Hoffman, Phillip W. *Simon Girty, Turncoat Hero: The Most Hated Man on the Early American Frontier*. Staunton, VA: American History Press, 2009.

James, Florence Bean, and Jean Freeman. *Fists Upon a Star: A Memoir of Love, Theatre, and Escape from McCarthyism*. Regina: University of Regina Press, 2013.

Klein, Bonnie Sherr. "Fierce Canadian Fears for Her
    Country." *Tyee*, May 27, 2013. https://thetyee.ca/
    Opinion/2013/05/27/Bonnie-Klein/.

Knowles, Norman. *Inventing the Loyalists: The Ontario
    Loyalist Tradition and the Creation of Usable Pasts.*
    Toronto: University of Toronto Press, 1997.

Leddy, Mary Jo. "Why Are We Here? A Meditation on
    Canada." Paper presented at the Catholic Health Alliance
    Conference, Charlottetown, May 10, 2017. www.chac.ca/
    conference/pastconferences/2017/docs/Mary Jo Leddy.

Merritt, John. "Remembering the Past, Legitimizing
    the Present: The Campaigns to Preserve the African
    Methodist Episcopal Church in Oro Township and
    Canadian Social Memory in the 1940s and the Present
    Day." MA thesis, Laurentian University, 2015.

Moore, Mavor. "Theatre Pioneer Was a Welcome U.S.
    Invader." Obituary of Florence Bean James. *Globe and
    Mail*, February 13, 1988, E1.

Newkirk, Anthony B. "Grace Lonergan Lorch (1903–1974)." In
    The Encyclopedia of Arkansas History and Culture. http://
    www.encyclopediaofarkansas.net/encyclopedia/entry-
    detail.aspx?entryID=8397.

Plaxton, Judy. "Lives Lived." *Globe and Mail*, May 15, 2015.
    https://www.theglobeandmail.com/life/facts-and-
    arguments/lives-lived-wilfred-joseph-theodore-sheffield-
    96/article24436004/.

Rattan, Chris. "The Plan to Decolonize Design." *NOW*, August
    30, 2017. https://nowtoronto.com/art-and-books/art/
    the-plan-to-decolonize-design/.

"Rita Deverell Fought Her Way on Stage—and 50 Years
    Later, She's Still Fighting." In *Up Close: A Special Series,*

with Lyndie Greenwood, CBC *Radio*, July 16, 2017. http://
www.cbc.ca/radio/docproject/upclose/rita-deverell-
fought-her-way-on-stage-and-50-years-later-she-s-still-
fighting-1.4207626.

Shepard, R. Bruce. *Deemed Unsuitable: Blacks from Oklahoma
Move to the Canadian Prairies in Search of Equality in
the Early 20th Century, Only to Find Racism in Their New
Home*. Kalispell, MT: Umbrella Press, 1997.

Sito, Tom. "The Disney Strike of 1941: How It Changed
Animation and Comics." Animation World Network
(awn.com). July 19, 2005. https://www.awn.com/
animationworld/disney-strike-1941-how-it-changed-
animation-comics.

Squires, Jessica. *Building Sanctuary: The Movement to Support
Vietnam War Resisters in Canada, 1965–73*. Vancouver:
UBC Press, 2013.

St. Onge, Anna. "Black History Month Featured Fonds: Lee
and Grace Lorch." *News from the Clara Thomas Archives
and Special Collections*, York University, February 24,
2012. http://deantiquate.blog.yorku.ca/2012/02/24/
bhm2012_leeandgracelorch/.

Truth and Reconciliation Commission. *Truth and
Reconciliation Commission of Canada: Calls to Action*.
Winnipeg: TRC, 2015. http://www.trc.ca/websites/
trcinstitution/File/2015/Findings/Calls_to_Action_
English2.pdf.

Tunstall, Elizabeth (Dori). "AIGA Respectful Design Video."
YouTube, October 17, 2016. https://www.youtube.com/
watch?v=SESVWI5aAHA.

———. "US Design Policy." *YouTube*, March 15, 2009. https://
www.youtube.com/watch?v=aSczizV8Eqc&spfreload=10.

———. "The Yin and Yang of Seduction and Production: Social Transitions of Ethnography between Seductive Play and Productive Force in Industry." *Ethnographic Praxis in Industry Conference Proceedings* 1 (2006): 125–37. ISSN 1559-890X. http://openresearch.ocadu.ca/id/eprint/1264/1/Tunstall_Yin_2006.pdf.

Tunstall, Elizabeth (Dori), and Casey Jones. "Beyond the Document: Living Institutions of US National Design Policy." *Design Management Review* 21, 4 (2010): 16–22. ISSN 15570614. http://openresearch.ocadu.ca/id/eprint/1279/1/Tunstall_Beyond_2010.pdf.

Whiteman, Carol. Interview with Sara Diamond. In "Creating Space for Authentic Voice in Canada's Screen Industry." EdD diss., Simon Fraser University, 2018.

Williams, Roger Neville. *The New Exiles: American War Resisters in Canada.* New York: Liveright Publishers, 1971.

Wilson, Carolynn. Interview with Naomi Norquay. In *Northern Terminus: The African Canadian History Journal* 8 (2011): 4–12. https://greyroots.com/sites/default/files/naomi_norquay_interview_with_carolynn_wilson_2011.pdf.

Wilson, William R. "Simon Girty: History's Realities Are Seldom Dull." *Historical Narratives of Early Canada.* http://www.uppercanadahistory.ca/ttuc/ttuc7.html.

"The Wilson Incident." *In Focus* (Rogers Television series), 2017. https://www.youtube.com/watch?v=m6GrxGeFkFY.

Winks, Robin. *The Blacks in Canada: A History.* 2nd ed. Montreal: McGill-Queen's University Press, 1997.

ABOUT THE AUTHOR

Rita Shelton Deverell was the twelfth holder of the Nancy's Chair in Women's Studies at Mount Saint Vincent University from July 2009 to June 2012. She has a BA in philosophy (Adelphi University), an MA in the history of religions (Columbia University), and an EdD on arts policy for children (OISE/University of Toronto).

Deverell has been a theatre artist, an independent television producer/director, a founder of Vision TV, and the first woman to lead a journalism program in Canada as acting director of the University of Regina's School of Journalism in the 1980s. In 2005, she concluded her term as news director at APTN, where she mentored her Indigenous successor. Deverell was also the CanWest Global Fellow at the University of Western Ontario and the Storyteller-in-Residence at Centennial College's Centre for Creative Communication.

In 2010, her full-length play *McCarthy and the Old Woman* had a first production by the School of Drama, University of Washington, which meant that its central character, Florence James, was portrayed on the same stage from which she had been blacklisted during the Cold War sixty years earlier. Deverell has been the author or editor of, or a major contributor to, seven books and the producer/director/writer of eight independent TV titles. In 2016, her multimedia e-learning kit *Women, Contemporary Aboriginal Issues, and Resistance* was acquired by the National Film Board's CAMPUS portal, giving it widespread North American distribution.

From 2015 to 2017, Deverell was a mentor for the Canadian Senior Artists Resource Network; in 2018 she was ACTRA's Woman of the Year for contributions to the arts and activism, and she has been made a life member of the union. Her many honours include two Geminis, the Black Women's Civic Engagement Leadership Award, and membership in the Canadian Association of Broadcasters Hall of Fame. Her 2005 Order of Canada citation says, in part, "Rita Deverell's career in journalism has been one of pioneering innovation and creativity. With an unceasing drive for social justice, she is one of the first Black women in Canada to be a television host and a network executive.…An inspiring mentor and teacher, she serves as a role model for young journalists and audiences alike."

THE REGINA COLLECTION

Named as a tribute to Saskatchewan's capital city with its rich history of boundary-defying innovation, *The Regina Collection* builds upon University of Regina Press's motto of "a voice for many peoples." Intimate in size and beautifully packaged, these books aim to tell the stories of those who have been caught up in social and political circumstances beyond their control.

To see other books in *The Regina Collection*, visit
WWW.UOFRPRESS.CA